lick it!

EASY, DAIRY-FREE RECIPES

creamy, dreamy
vegan ice creams
your mouth will love

Cathe Olson

BOOK PUBLISHING COMPANY
Summertown, Tennessee

Library of Congress Cataloging-in-Publication Data

Olson, Cathe.
  Lick it! : creamy, dreamy vegan ice creams your mouth will love / by Cathe Olson.
    p. cm.
  Includes bibliographical references and index.
  ISBN 978-1-57067-237-8 (alk. paper)
1. Ice cream, ices, etc. 2. Non-dairy frozen desserts. 3. Vegan cookery.
I. Title.

  TX795.O58 2009
  641.8'62--dc22

                                            2009003946

Cover and interior design: *Aerocraft Charter Art Service*

Printed in Canada

Book Publishing Company
P.O. Box 99
Summertown, TN 38483
888-260-8458
www.bookpubco.com

ISBN-13 978-1-57067-237-8

17 16 15 14 13 12 11 10 09   1 2 3 4 5 6 7 8 9

Book Publishing Co. is a member of Green Press Initiative. We chose to print this title on paper with postconsumer recycled content, processed without chlorine, which saved the following natural resources:

63 trees

2,930 pounds of solid waste

22,816 gallons of wastewater

5,497 pounds of greenhouse gases

44 million BTU of total energy

For more information, visit www.greenpressinitiative.org.

Paper calculations from Environmental Defense Paper Calculator, www.papercalculator.org

contents

I LOVE ICE ICE CREAM!

preface

I admit it. I love ice cream. Always have—and probably always will. Some of my fondest childhood memories are of my whole family walking downtown to get cones on hot summer nights. As a teen, I worked after school at an ice-cream parlor, always trying to invent a new float or sundae. In my twenties, working as a secretary, I ate mint chip ice cream for breakfast every morning (not that I'm recommending that!).

As an adult, my love for ice cream hasn't dimmed. In fact, when I stopped eating dairy products, it was never the cheese or butter I missed—it was the ice cream. I know there are plenty of nondairy substitutes out there, but to me they just don't cut it. They're too icy, oversweet, and just don't have that rich creaminess I crave.

I started making my own nondairy ice creams several years ago, and a friend suggested that I put my recipes into a book. I wasn't sure I could come up with a whole book of nondairy ice-cream recipes, but I decided to give it a try—with the condition that I'd only do it if every recipe tasted as good as (or better than!) the very best dairy ice creams. As I worked on recipe after recipe, testing them on family and friends (and on their families and friends), no one even suspected that my ice "creams" weren't made the regular way, with cow's milk and cream. They raved about the flavor combinations, the rich taste, and the creamy texture. That's when I knew I had to share these recipes.

Whether you're avoiding dairy products for health, environmental, or ethical reasons, you can now have fabulous ice cream anytime you want. I hope you enjoy eating these treats as much as I enjoyed creating them.

acknowledgments

I am so thankful to all the people who helped this book come to fruition. First, I'd like to thank all of my friends and my daughters' friends who tirelessly tested my recipes, especially the Pock, Simon, and Collins families. Your discerning taste buds helped me so much. Thanks also to my wonderful in-laws, Richard and Lynn Olson, who have been so supportive of all my cookbooks and have tested many, many of my creations and never once complained.

Second, I'd like to thank the whole staff at Book Publishing Company, who enthusiastically embraced my cookbook, especially Bob and Cynthia Holzapfel, who turned my vision into reality. I am deeply indebted to Jo Stepaniak, who is one of my heroes as an author and animal activist. Thanks for getting rid of all of the rough edges in my manuscript and fine-tuning it into this wonderful cookbook.

More than anyone, I want to thank my family. Aimie and Emily, my amazing daughters, you were such great tasters and I appreciate your help creating many of these recipes. Thanks for inviting your friends over again and again for tasting parties and always wholeheartedly supporting my efforts to get every recipe just right. Gary, my dear husband, I can always count on you for an honest opinion and that means a lot to me. Thanks for supporting all my dreams and endeavors.

getting started

Homemade nondairy ice cream is surprisingly easy to make and tastes so much better than anything you can buy in a store. Even dairy eaters agree that these recipes are as delicious and satisfying as any ice cream they've had. You'll find all your favorite traditional flavors plus a tempting variety of exotic and gourmet flavors made with herbs, spices, and liqueurs. The best part about making your own ice cream is that you can adjust the sweeteners and flavorings to your own taste—so don't be afraid to experiment and have fun.

the ice-cream base

The mixture of milks, sweeteners, and other ingredients that will be frozen into ice cream is called the ice-cream *base*. The base should be very cold before it is put in the ice-cream maker or the ice cream will come out too soft. Most recipes require the base to be chilled in the refrigerator for several hours before it is frozen in the ice-cream maker. To chill the ice cream base more quickly, put it in the freezer for about an hour. Ice-cream bases can be kept for up to three days in the refrigerator.

hardening

Ice cream fresh from the machine will be fairly soft—the perfect consistency for eating. If you prefer a harder ice cream, transfer the ice cream to a freezerproof container, cover it, and freeze it for several hours until it reaches your desired firmness. Sorbets and ice creams with liqueurs or mix-ins will usually require some hardening in the freezer.

storage

Homemade ice creams have a shorter shelf life than commercially prepared versions made with stabilizers and preservatives. The ice creams in this book will keep for about two months in the freezer.

Store your homemade ice cream in a freezerproof container with a tight-fitting lid. I prefer glass containers. I've found glass bowls with plastic lids in all sizes at kitchen supply stores. High-quality plastic containers can also be used.

Since thawing and refreezing ice cream causes its quality to deteriorate, pack homemade ice cream into smaller containers and try to fill them to within one-half inch of the rim. A piece of parchment paper laid directly on top of ice creams that don't fill a container will help to prevent the formation of ice crystals on the surface. Your freezer should be set to 0 degrees F.

tempering

Homemade ice creams freeze more solidly than commercially prepared versions. After the ice cream is completely frozen, leave it at room temperature for ten to thirty minutes (depending on the quantity), until it is soft enough to scoop. This is called *tempering*. Ice-cream cakes and pies should also be tempered before they are sliced. If your kitchen is very warm, tempering the ice cream or dessert in the refrigerator (for thirty to sixty minutes) will give a more even result.

making ice cream with a machine

Ice cream is formed by the constant stirring of the ice-cream base as it freezes. The churning breaks up the ice crystals to create a smooth, creamy product. Although you can do it by hand (see instructions on p. 3), an ice-cream maker makes the process easy. There are several types of home ice-cream machines that can be found at department stores and cookware stores; they can also be purchased from online retailers.

No matter which ice-cream maker you choose, you'll need a machine that holds one and a half quarts to make the recipes in this book. If you have a larger-capacity ice-cream maker, increase the ingredient amounts to obtain the correct quantity for your machine. The ice-cream recipes in this book yield about one quart of ice cream, though some will make slightly more or less. Feel free to alter the recipes, but keep in mind that you need to use between three and four cups of base or your ice cream will not freeze properly.

MACHINES USING SALT AND ICE

Machines requiring salt and ice, either electric or hand cranked, can be fun to use and produce delicious ice cream. They are usually available in either a four- or six-quart size, which is great when you need ice cream for a lot of people. Because they require salt and ice, however, they are not necessarily convenient for regular use.

MACHINES USING PREFROZEN CANISTERS

Electric ice-cream makers using prefrozen canisters are relatively inexpensive and very easy to use. Companies that make reliable cooking appliances, like Cuisinart and KitchenAid, are good choices when it comes to this type of ice-cream maker. Donvier makes a nonelectric version, which is fun for kids. For both the electric and nonelectric models, the gel-filled canister needs to be frozen eight to twenty-two hours before you can make ice cream. I find it most convenient to just store the canister permanently in my freezer—that way I can make ice cream whenever the mood strikes me. The disadvantage, of course, is the space the canister takes up in the freezer. I recommend getting a second gel canister so you can make two flavors at a time—especially if you want to make a terrine or layered ice-cream dessert.

MACHINES USING BUILT-IN FREON UNITS

Countertop machines with their own freezing units are convenient and require no advance preparation. They do take up quite a bit of counter space and are expensive.

making ice cream without a machine

Any of the ice creams in this book can be made without an ice-cream machine, though the process requires a lot more time and effort.

Place the well-chilled ice-cream base into a fairly shallow (no deeper than two inches) freezerproof pan or dish. Cover and put it the freezer. After about forty-five minutes, check the base. When it is partially frozen, remove it from the freezer and beat it vigorously with a fork or a handheld mixer. Beat it until it is smooth, breaking up any frozen sections. Then return it to the freezer. Continue to beat the ice cream every thirty minutes and return it to the freezer. Repeat this process until the ice cream is frozen. The freezing and beating method takes two to four hours.

tips for success

- Always start with cold ingredients or the ice cream will not freeze firmly enough. For many recipes, this means you'll have to start the preparation in advance—either the night before or the morning of the day you plan to make the ice cream. Ice-cream bases can be stored in the refrigerator for up to three days.

- Using frozen fruit for recipes that call for fruit will produce a cold base that can be frozen in an ice-cream maker immediately. For some recipes, you'll have to partially thaw the frozen fruit or the base will be too thick to process in a blender.

- When testing a base for sweetness prior to freezing it, keep in mind that the ice cream will be slightly less sweet after it is frozen. This is because the formation of ice crystals during the freezing process will slightly dilute the flavor of the ice cream.

- When you use an ice-cream maker with a gel canister, make sure the canister is completely frozen before you freeze the ice cream. Depending on the temperature of your freezer, it can take eight to twenty-two hours for a gel canister to freeze completely. Shake the canister to determine whether it is completely frozen. If you hear liquid moving, it is not ready. Have the ice-cream maker set up and all ingredients and equipment ready before you remove the gel canister from the freezer, as it will defrost quickly.

- When adding mix-ins like chips or nuts, wait until the ice cream is fairly firm, about five minutes before it is completely frozen. Add the mix-ins through the top spout with the ice-cream maker running, and process the mixture until the ice cream is firm. Ice cream with mix-ins will often be soft and require hardening in the freezer.

- Leftover ice creams and sorbets make excellent ice pops—and when they are used this way, you don't have to worry about tempering. After you fill the pop mold, poke the ice cream a few times with a butter knife to get out the air bubbles, and then add more ice cream, if necessary.

ingredients

chocolate

Dairy-free chocolate can be found at natural food stores and well-stocked supermarkets; it is also available from many online retailers. You can't always tell from the front of the package whether the product contains dairy, so it's best to check the label to see if milk products are listed.

chocolate chips. I prefer mini chocolate chips in ice cream; standard-size chips don't mix in very well. If you like even smaller chips, use a sturdy, sharp knife to finely chop a dark or semisweet chocolate bar. (Don't use a food processor, as it will turn the chocolate to powder.) If you microwave the bar for a few seconds, it won't crumble as much when you chop it.

chocolate syrup and sauce. Use organic, dairy-free chocolate syrup or make your own (see p. 117).

cocoa powder. Use unsweetened cocoa powder, not drinking or sipping chocolate.

dark and semisweet chocolate. Use sweetened baking chocolate or good-quality chocolate bars.

unsweetened chocolate. Use unsweetened baking chocolate. It usually comes in packages containing one-ounce squares, so it is easy to measure.

white chocolate. Most white chocolate contains dairy products, so be sure to check the label. Cocoa butter should be listed as one of the top ingredients.

cones and toppings

When purchasing cones and sprinkles, syrups, and other toppings, be sure to check the package label to see if any dairy products or derivatives are listed.

flavorings

Always have a bottle of vanilla extract on hand, because a large percentage of the recipes call for it. I prefer pure vanilla extract for the best flavor. Other extracts and spices used in the recipes can be found at the supermarket. You may have some of the fresh herbs used in these ice creams growing in your garden. If not, look for them at your local farmers' market or grocery store.

fruit

Use organic fruit whenever possible, as most fruit is heavily treated with pesticides, mold retardants, and other chemicals. The fruit should be ripe but not overripe. Frozen fruit works fine in most recipes and has the added benefit of creating a cold base that can be processed immediately, rather than needing to be chilled. In the summer, when fruit is plentiful, buy extra to freeze for later use.

how to freeze fruit

Clean the fruit and remove the peel, pits, or hulls, if necessary. Slice the fruit, arrange it in a single layer on a baking sheet, and place it in the freezer for one to two hours. When it is frozen, transfer the fruit to a freezer container or a heavy-duty zipper-lock bag and store it in the freezer. Frozen fruit will keep for three to six months.

nondairy milks and creams

coconut milk. Many of the ice creams in this book call for coconut milk to give them the rich creaminess usually found only in dairy ice cream. Use canned, full-fat coconut milk, not lite. For a special treat, make coconut milk from a fresh coconut. It's a lot of work but quite delicious.

nut milks. Almond and other nut milks work fine as a soymilk replacement. Cashew milk is rich and creamy and is featured in several recipes in place of coconut milk.

rice milk. Rice milk is slightly less rich than soymilk but works in any recipes calling for nondairy milk. Always use plain rice milk unless otherwise specified in the recipe.

how to convert the recipes to include dairy products

If you prefer to use dairy products and picked up this book because you couldn't resist the variety of recipes it contains, you'll be happy to know that you can easily replace the nondairy ingredients with dairy alternatives. Substitute heavy cream for coconut milk, whole cow's milk for soymilk, and dairy yogurt for soy yogurt.

how to make coconut milk

Coconuts are available year-round at most supermarkets and natural food stores. Choose a coconut that is heavy for its size and full of liquid—you can tell by shaking it. To open the coconut, use a large nail or ice pick to pierce two of the soft, black "eyes" at the top of the coconut. Drain and reserve the liquid (called *coconut water*).

Preheat the oven to 350 degrees F and bake the drained coconut for about 20 minutes. Alternatively, put it in the freezer for an hour. Either method will make the shell brittle so that when you whack it with a hammer, it should break in two.

Use a sharp knife to separate the meat from the shell. Peel off any dark brown skin clinging to the white meat. Mince the meat in a food processor fitted with a metal blade. You'll need to stop occasionally to scrape down the sides of the work bowl until the coconut meat is evenly minced. A medium coconut will yield $3\frac{1}{4}$ to 4 cups of meat.

Now you can make the milk. Measure the coconut water and add enough plain water to it to equal $1\frac{1}{2}$ cups. Transfer to a blender along with the coconut meat. Pulse and process until smooth, adding more water, if necessary, to facilitate processing.

soymilk. Soymilk is not rich enough on its own to make ice cream, but it works well mixed with coconut milk or tofu. I use organic, unsweetened soymilk. If you are avoiding soy, rice milk will work fine in these recipes, though the ice cream will be slightly less creamy. Soy creamer is used occasionally in the book, mostly in sauces.

nuts

Almonds, cashews, pecans, pistachios, walnuts, and other nuts used in the recipes should be raw and unsalted unless otherwise specified. Some recipes call for toasted nuts, which are more flavorful.

how to toast nuts

To toast nuts, put them in a dry skillet on medium-low heat. Stir occasionally, until they begin to pop and give off a nutty aroma. Immediately remove the nuts from the skillet (so they don't burn) and transfer them to a plate. Cool the nuts completely before adding them to ice cream.

spirits

Liqueurs and spirits add flavor and depth to ice creams and sorbets. However, a little goes a long way; too much can overpower ice cream. When alcohol is added to an ice-cream base, it takes longer to freeze, and the finished ice cream will be soft. In fact, if too much alcohol is added, the base won't freeze at all, so it's best to stick to the measurements given. If possible, harden ice creams that contain liqueur in the freezer for several hours before serving. Not only will this produce a firmer ice cream, it will give the flavors a chance to develop and harmonize.

sweeteners

I prefer natural sweeteners that contain some nutrients and are less refined. Pay attention to how ripe and sweet the fruit is when you are using it in a base. If the fruit is very sweet, less sweetener may be needed than is called for in the recipe; if the fruit is tart, more sweetener may be needed. I don't use and don't recommend artificial sweeteners.

agave syrup. Agave syrup is extracted from the agave cactus. It is metabolized more slowly than sugar and is less likely to cause blood-sugar fluctuations. It is a liquid sweetener, similar in consistency to honey and maple syrup; but, unlike those sweeteners, agave syrup has a very mild flavor that will not overpower your ice cream.

granulated sugar. For recipes calling for granulated sugar, I recommend using organically grown unbleached cane sugar, also called evaporated cane juice. Refined white cane sugar is highly processed and is often filtered using animal bone char. When a darker sugar is required, use organic brown, raw, or turbinado sugar.

maple syrup. Although I love maple syrup for baking, its flavor is very strong in ice creams. I only use maple syrup in ice creams if I really want a maple flavor. Maple syrup works well in sauces.

liqueur flavors

Liqueurs add flavor and depth to ice creams and sorbets. Table 1 lists the flavors various liqueurs impart.

TABLE 1
Liquers and their flavors

LIQUEUR	FLAVOR
Amaretto	almond
Chambord	blackberry
Cointreau	orange
Frangelico	hazelnut
Godiva	chocolate
Grand Marnier	orange
Kahlúa	coffee
Kirsch	cherry
Limoncello	lemon-lime
Pama	pomegranate
Triple Sec	orange

ice-cream parlor favorites

TRADITIONAL AND EXOTIC FLAVORS

1

This section contains ice-cream recipes with the same range of flavors that you would find at a good ice-cream parlor, so you can have all the ice creams you enjoyed as a child—but without the dairy! You'll also find some exotic flavors made with herbs and spices for more adventurous taste buds. All of the recipes require the ice-cream base to be chilled before it is frozen in an ice-cream maker, so be sure to allow extra time.

A good, basic vanilla ice cream is a must. This recipe is easy and delicious. It's perfect for everything from hot fudge sundaes to topping your favorite pie or crisp. It's great on its own too.

vanilla ICE CREAM

1 (14-ounce) can full-fat coconut milk

1 1/4 cups soymilk or other nondairy milk

1/2 cup granulated sugar or agave syrup

1 tablespoon vanilla extract

Place all of the ingredients in a medium bowl and whisk until well combined. Cover and chill in the refrigerator for at least 2 hours. Then freeze in an ice-cream maker according to the manufacturer's directions.

cherry-vanilla ice cream: About 5 minutes before the end of the freezing time, when the ice cream is almost to the firmness you desire, add 1/2 to 3/4 cup of chopped dark cherries. Process for 5 more minutes, or until the ice cream reaches the desired consistency.

chocolate chip ice cream: About 5 minutes before the end of the freezing time, when the ice cream is almost to the firmness you desire, add 1/2 cup of mini dark or semisweet chocolate chips or chopped chocolate. Process for 5 more minutes, or until the ice cream reaches the desired consistency.

cookies-and-cream ice cream: About 5 minutes before the end of the freezing time, when the ice cream is almost to the firmness you desire, add 1/2 cup of crushed crème-filled chocolate sandwich cookies. Process for 5 more minutes, or until the ice cream reaches the desired consistency.

peppermint stick ice cream: About 5 minutes before the end of the freezing time, when the ice cream is almost to the firmness you desire, add 1/2 cup of crushed peppermint candies. Process for 5 more minutes, or until the ice cream reaches the desired consistency.

vanilla-fudge brownie ice cream: When the ice cream is done, turn off the ice-cream maker and remove the churn. Gently fold in 1/2 to 3/4 cup of crumbled brownie chunks. Harden the ice cream in the freezer for several hours, or until it reaches the desired firmness.

Marbling ice cream can be a little tricky without the special machine that ice-cream manufacturers have. If you stir in the chocolate, it will just blend with the base and won't stay separate. The layering technique I use is easy and produces a nice marbled effect when the ice cream is scooped. This ice cream will need to harden in the freezer for a few hours, so be sure to plan ahead.

vanilla-fudge marble ICE CREAM

VANILLA BASE

1 (14-ounce) **can full-fat coconut milk**

1¼ cups soymilk or other nondairy milk

½ cup granulated sugar or agave syrup

1 tablespoon vanilla extract

FUDGE SAUCE

¼ cup soymilk or rice milk

½ cup semisweet chocolate chips

To make the base, place the coconut milk, soymilk, sugar, and vanilla extract in a medium bowl and whisk until well combined. Cover and chill in the refrigerator for at least 2 hours.

To make the sauce, pour the soymilk into a small saucepan and place on medium-low heat until it almost comes to a boil. Remove from the heat and whisk in the chocolate chips until smooth. Chill in the refrigerator for at least 1 hour.

Freeze the chilled base in an ice-cream maker according to the manufacturer's directions. Put a 1-quart freezerproof container in the freezer for 15 minutes. Remove the fudge sauce from the refrigerator and have it ready. Spread a layer of the base in the chilled container. Drizzle a layer of fudge sauce over the base. Continue layering in this fashion until all the base and fudge sauce are used, finishing with a layer of the base. Freeze for several hours, or until firm.

butterscotch ripple ice cream: Use ¾ cup chilled Butterscotch Sauce (p. 118) in place of the fudge sauce.

This is a delicious treat when you have a little more time (and money, because vanilla beans can be expensive) to spend. It's worth it though—nothing beats the taste of real vanilla beans. Look for soft beans, as the brittle ones are harder to work with.

vanilla bean ICE CREAM

MAKES 1 QUART

1½ cups soymilk or other nondairy milk

1 whole vanilla bean

½ cup granulated sugar or agave syrup

1 (14-ounce) can full-fat coconut milk

1 teaspoon vanilla extract

Pour the soymilk into a small saucepan. Slice the vanilla bean in half lengthwise using a sharp knife or shears. Working with one half at a time, hold the pod over the pan and scrape out the seeds with a blunt knife (a butter knife works well) into the soymilk. Stir the seeds and pod into the soymilk and bring to a boil on medium heat. Reduce the heat to low and simmer for 15 minutes, stirring occasionally.

Remove from the heat and let rest for 5 minutes. Discard the vanilla pods and any skin that may have formed on the soymilk. Pour into a heat-proof bowl and whisk in the sugar until it is dissolved. Then whisk in the coconut milk and vanilla extract. Cover and chill in the refrigerator for at least 3 hours. Then freeze in an ice-cream maker according to the manufacturer's directions.

Vanilla ice cream marbled with blackberry preserves and studded with dark chocolate truffles—I should have called this heaven in a bowl! If you don't have blackberry jam, use raspberry or strawberry.

vanilla-blackberry truffle ICE CREAM

MAKES 1 QUART

1 (14-ounce) can full-fat coconut milk

1¼ cups soymilk or other nondairy milk

½ cup granulated sugar or agave syrup

1 tablespoon vanilla extract

¾ cup chopped Chocolate Truffles (p. 126) made with Chambord liqueur

⅓ cup blackberry jam

Place the coconut milk, soymilk, sugar, and vanilla extract in a medium bowl and whisk until well combined. Cover and chill in the refrigerator for at least 2 hours. Then freeze in an ice-cream maker according to the manufacturer's directions.

Put a 1-quart freezerproof container in the freezer for 15 minutes. Remove the churn from the ice-cream maker and gently fold in the truffles.

Scoop about 1 cup of the ice cream into the chilled container. Spread one-third of the jam over the ice cream. Continue layering in this fashion until all the ice cream and jam are used, finishing with a layer of the ice cream. Freeze for several hours, or until firm.

If you're like me and love bites of raw cookie dough as much as a baked cookie, this flavor will be irresistible.

chocolate chip cookie dough ICE CREAM

VANILLA BASE

1 (14-ounce) **can full-fat coconut milk**

1¼ cups soymilk or other nondairy milk

½ cup granulated sugar or agave syrup

1 tablespoon vanilla extract

CHOCOLATE CHIP
COOKIE DOUGH

3 tablespoons maple syrup

3 tablespoons vegetable oil

½ teaspoon vanilla extract

¾ cups whole wheat pastry or unbleached white flour

Dash salt

¼ to ⅓ cup mini dark or semisweet chocolate chips or chopped chocolate

To make the base, place the coconut milk, soymilk, sugar, and vanilla extract in a medium bowl and whisk until well combined. Cover and chill in the refrigerator for at least 2 hours.

To make the cookie dough, place the maple syrup, oil, and vanilla extract in a medium bowl and whisk until well combined. Stir in the flour and salt to form a stiff dough. Fold in the chocolate chips. Line a small baking sheet or plate with parchment paper (I use the baking tray from my toaster oven). Press the dough onto the sheet until it is about ¼ inch thick. Using a knife or pizza cutter, score the dough lengthwise into ½-inch strips. Then score the dough widthwise to create bite-size chunks. Put the dough in the freezer for at least 30 minutes and keep it frozen until the ice cream is made.

When the ice-cream base is chilled, freeze it in an ice-cream maker according to the manufacturer's directions. Remove the churn and fold in the cookie dough chunks. Transfer to a freezer-proof container and freeze for 2 hours, or until the ice cream reaches the desired firmness.

There's something about ice-cold mint that really awakens the taste buds. This is another flavor that tastes great in a hot fudge sundae, or try it as a filling for Grasshopper Pie (see table 2, p. 73).

mint ICE CREAM

MAKES 1 QUART

1 (14-ounce) can full-fat coconut milk

1¼ cups soymilk or other nondairy milk

½ cup granulated sugar or agave syrup

2 teaspoons peppermint extract

Place all of the ingredients in a medium bowl and whisk until well combined. Cover and chill in the refrigerator for at least 2 hours. Then freeze in an ice-cream maker according to the manufacturer's directions.

mint–chocolate chip ice cream: About 5 minutes before the end of the freezing time, when the ice cream is almost to the firmness you desire, add ½ cup of mini dark or semisweet chocolate chips or chopped chocolate. Process for 5 more minutes, or until the ice cream reaches the desired consistency.

mint cookies-and-cream ice cream: About 5 minutes before the end of the freezing time, when the ice cream is almost to the firmness you desire, add ½ cup of crushed crème-filled chocolate sandwich cookies. Process for 5 more minutes, or until the ice cream reaches the desired consistency.

Chocolate ice cream was one of my biggest challenges. It had to be rich, creamy, smooth, and very chocolaty. This is it!

chocolate ICE CREAM

1 ¼ cups soymilk or other nondairy milk

⅓ cup granulated sugar

2 tablespoons unsweetened cocoa powder

3 ounces dark chocolate

3 ounces semisweet chocolate

1 (14-ounce) can full-fat coconut milk

2 teaspoons vanilla extract

Combine the soymilk, sugar, and cocoa powder in a medium saucepan and whisk until smooth. Warm on medium heat until the soymilk begins to simmer. Remove from the heat.

Put the dark and semisweet chocolate in a heatproof bowl. Pour the hot soymilk mixture over the chocolate and stir until smooth. Whisk in the coconut milk and vanilla extract. Cover and chill in the refrigerator for at least 3 hours. Then freeze in an ice-cream maker according to the manufacturer's directions.

chocolate-almond ice cream: Add ½ teaspoon of almond extract along with the vanilla extract. About 5 minutes before the end of the freezing time, when the ice cream is almost to the firmness you desire, add ½ cup of chopped toasted almonds. Process for 5 more minutes, or until the ice cream reaches the desired consistency.

chocolate–chocolate chip ice cream: About 5 minutes before the end of the freezing time, when the ice cream is almost to the firmness you desire, add ½ cup of mini dark or semisweet chocolate chips or chopped chocolate. Process for 5 more minutes, or until the ice cream reaches the desired consistency.

chocolate-hazelnut ice cream: Add 2 tablespoons of Frangelico liqueur along with the vanilla extract. About 5 minutes before the end of the freezing time, when the ice cream is almost to the firmness you desire, add ½ cup of skinned and chopped toasted hazelnuts (see p. 7). Process for 5 more minutes. Transfer the ice cream to a freezerproof container and freeze until it reaches the desired consistency.

chocolate truffle ice cream: Prepare Chocolate Truffles (p. 126) with the liqueur of your choice and place them in the refrigerator to chill. When the ice cream is done, turn off the ice-cream maker and remove the churn. Chop the truffles and gently fold them into the ice cream. Transfer the ice cream to a freezerproof container and freeze until it reaches the desired consistency.

mexican chocolate ice cream: Add 1 teaspoon of ground cinnamon and $\frac{1}{4}$ teaspoon of chili powder along with the vanilla extract.

mint-chocolate ice cream: Add 1 teaspoon of peppermint extract and reduce the vanilla extract to 1 teaspoon.

orange-chocolate ice cream: Add $\frac{1}{2}$ teaspoon of orange extract and reduce the vanilla extract to 1 teaspoon.

rocky road ice cream: When the ice cream is done, turn off the ice-cream maker and remove the churn. Stir in $\frac{1}{2}$ cup of vegan mini marshmallows (or diced large marshmallows) and $\frac{1}{2}$ cup of chopped walnuts. Transfer to a freezerproof container and freeze until it reaches the desired consistency.

This luscious ice cream is made without coconut milk but is still extremely rich and very chocolaty. This is what I serve when I host a Moms' Night Out at my house.

chocolate mousse ICE CREAM

MAKES 1 QUART

1½ cups chocolate rice milk or soymilk

1½ cups semisweet chocolate chips (one 10-ounce package)

1 (12-ounce) package firm silken tofu

3 tablespoons Amaretto liqueur

1 teaspoon vanilla extract

¼ teaspoon almond extract

Pour the rice milk into a small saucepan and warm on low heat until it just begins to simmer. Remove from the heat, add the chocolate chips, and whisk until they are melted and the mixture is smooth. Transfer to a blender or food processor and add the tofu, liqueur, and extracts. Process until smooth. Cover and chill in the refrigerator for at least 2 hours. Then freeze in an ice-cream maker according to the manufacturer's directions.

Rich dark chocolate tinged with fresh red raspberries—a wonderful flavor combination. To make this even more decadent, add a couple of tablespoons of Chambord liqueur.

chocolate-raspberry ICE CREAM

1 (14-ounce) **can full-fat coconut milk**

½ cup plus 2 tablespoons granulated sugar

5 tablespoons unsweetened cocoa powder

2 cups raspberries

Place the coconut milk, sugar, and cocoa powder in a medium saucepan and whisk until well combined. Warm on medium-low heat until the mixture just begins to simmer and get foamy. Remove from the heat and stir in the raspberries. Let rest for 20 minutes.

Pour the mixture into a blender or food processor and process until smooth. Place a fine-mesh strainer over a medium bowl (or, to save on dishwashing, over the saucepan you used to heat the coconut milk). Pour the blended mixture into the strainer and press it through to remove the seeds. Cover and chill in the refrigerator for at least 3 hours. Then freeze in an ice-cream maker according to the manufacturer's directions.

This ice cream is ultracreamy, with a flavor reminiscent of whipped cream. It works beautifully in a hot fudge sundae or served with a slice of chocolate cake.

white chocolate ICE CREAM

MAKES 1 QUART

1¼ cups soymilk or other nondairy milk

¾ cup white chocolate chips or chopped white chocolate (about 6 ounces)

1 (14-ounce) can full-fat coconut milk

2 teaspoons vanilla extract

Pour the soymilk into a medium saucepan. Add the chocolate and warm on low heat, whisking occasionally, until the chocolate melts. Pour the mixture into a heatproof bowl. Whisk in the coconut milk and vanilla extract. Cover and chill in the refrigerator for at least 3 hours. Then freeze in an ice-cream maker according to the manufacturer's directions.

This tastes just like the butterscotch hard candy I loved as a kid.

butterscotch ICE CREAM

MAKES 1 QUART

1 (14-ounce) can full-fat coconut milk

1¼ cups soymilk or other nondairy milk

¾ cup Butterscotch Sauce (p. 118)

Place all of the ingredients in a medium bowl and whisk until well combined. Cover and chill in the refrigerator for at least 2 hours. Then freeze in an ice-cream maker according to the manufacturer's directions.

I love the pure coffee flavor in this ice cream, but be warned—this ice cream can keep you up at night. If you're sensitive to caffeine, use decaffeinated coffee or a powdered coffee substitute.

coffee ICE CREAM

MAKES 1 QUART

1 (14-ounce) can full-fat coconut milk

1¼ cups soymilk or other nondairy milk

½ cup granulated sugar or agave syrup

2 tablespoons instant coffee granules or powdered coffee substitute

1 teaspoon vanilla extract

Place all of the ingredients in a medium bowl and whisk until well combined. Cover and chill in the refrigerator for at least 2 hours. Then freeze in an ice-cream maker according to the manufacturer's directions.

coffee–fudge brownie ice cream: When the ice cream is done, turn off the ice-cream maker and remove the churn. Gently fold in ½ to ¾ cup of crumbled brownie chunks. Transfer the ice cream to a freezerproof container and freeze until it reaches the desired consistency.

There's nothing like the mixture of chocolate and coffee to give your taste buds a good buzz.

mocha ICE CREAM

MAKES 1 QUART

1 ¼ cups soymilk or other nondairy milk

2 tablespoons instant coffee granules or powdered coffee substitute

⅓ cup granulated sugar

3 ounces dark chocolate

3 ounces semisweet chocolate

1 (14-ounce) can full-fat coconut milk

2 teaspoons vanilla extract

Place the soymilk, instant coffee, and sugar into a medium saucepan and whisk until smooth. Warm on medium heat until the mixture just begins to simmer. Remove from the heat.

Put the dark and semisweet chocolate in a heatproof bowl. Pour the hot soymilk mixture over the chocolate and whisk until smooth. Whisk in the coconut milk and vanilla extract. Cover and chill in the refrigerator for at least 3 hours. Then freeze in an ice-cream maker according to the manufacturer's directions.

mocha-chip ice cream: About 5 minutes before the end of the freezing time, when the ice cream is almost to the firmness you desire, add ½ cup of mini dark or semisweet chocolate chips or chopped chocolate. Process for 5 more minutes, or until the ice cream reaches the desired consistency.

mocha-almond ice cream: About 5 minutes before the end of the freezing time, when the ice cream is almost to the firmness you desire, add ½ cup of chopped toasted almonds. Process for 5 more minutes, or until the ice cream reaches the desired consistency.

mocha-almond-fudge ice cream: Follow the directions for Vanilla–Fudge Marble Ice Cream (p. 11), but use Mocha-Almond Ice Cream (above) instead of the vanilla base.

22   LICK IT!

This is a flavor kids love—especially when it is marbled with fudge sauce or jam, as in the variations that follow.

peanut butter ICE CREAM

1 (14-ounce) **can full-fat coconut milk**

1 cup soymilk or other nondairy milk

½ cup granulated sugar or agave syrup

6 tablespoons creamy peanut butter

½ cup chopped roasted peanuts (salted or unsalted; optional)

Place the coconut milk, soymilk, sugar, and peanut butter in a medium bowl and whisk until well combined. Cover and chill in the refrigerator for at least 2 hours. Then freeze in an ice-cream maker according to the manufacturer's directions.

About 5 minutes before the end of the freezing time, when the ice cream is almost to the firmness you desire, add the optional peanuts. Process for 5 more minutes, or until the ice cream reaches the desired consistency.

peanut butter–chocolate chip ice cream: Add ½ cup of mini dark or semisweet chocolate chips or chopped chocolate instead of the chopped peanuts.

peanut butter–fudge marble ice cream: Follow the directions for Vanilla–Fudge Marble Ice Cream (p. 11), but use Peanut Butter Ice Cream instead of the vanilla base.

peanut butter and jelly ice cream: Follow the directions for the Vanilla–Fudge Marble Ice Cream (p. 11), but use Peanut Butter Ice Cream instead of the vanilla base and use ½ cup of jelly or jam instead of the fudge sauce.

This flavor requires some advance planning. Start soaking the raisins and chilling the soymilk the night before you plan to serve this ice cream. Freeze it in the morning and by the afternoon the ice cream will be ready to dish up.

rum raisin ICE CREAM

MAKES 1 GENEROUS QUART

¾ cup raisins

¼ cup dark rum

1 (14-ounce) can full-fat coconut milk

1 cup soymilk or other nondairy milk

½ cup granulated sugar or agave syrup

Combine the raisins and rum in a small bowl. Cover and let soak for 3 to 12 hours.

Place the coconut milk, soymilk, and sugar in a medium bowl and whisk until well combined. Cover and chill in the refrigerator for at least 2 hours. Then freeze in an ice-cream maker according to the manufacturer's directions. Freeze for 20 to 25 minutes, or until fairly firm.

Add the soaked raisins (and any remaining rum in the bowl) and process for 5 more minutes, or until the raisins are evenly mixed in. You may need to stop the ice-cream maker and mix with a spatula a few times if the churn gets clogged. The finished ice cream will be quite soft. Transfer it to a freezerproof container and freeze for several hours, or until it reaches the desired consistency.

NOTE: In addition to hardening the ice cream, the freezing time will allow the flavor to develop.

This ice cream reminds me of New England, where I grew up. We always had plenty of maple syrup from Vermont. If you can find it, use Grade B maple syrup to give this ice cream a richer flavor.

maple-walnut ICE CREAM

MAKES 1 QUART

½ cup chopped walnuts

1 (14-ounce) can full-fat coconut milk

1¼ cups soymilk or other nondairy milk

½ cup maple syrup

Toast the walnuts in a dry skillet on medium-low heat until they turn golden and emit a nutty aroma. Cool the nuts slightly. Then put them in the freezer to use later.

Place the coconut milk, soymilk, and maple syrup in a medium bowl and whisk until well combined. Cover and chill in the refrigerator for at least 2 hours. Then freeze in an ice-cream maker according to the manufacturer's directions.

About 5 minutes before the end of the freezing time, when the ice cream is almost to the firmness you desire, add the walnuts. Process for 5 more minutes, or until the ice cream reaches the desired consistency.

Rather than coconut milk, cashews and walnuts give this ice cream its richness.

double nut-maple ICE CREAM

⅔ cup walnuts, toasted and cooled

1 cup raw cashews

2 cups water

⅔ cup maple syrup

Place the walnuts and cashews in a blender and grind them into a fine powder. Add the water and maple syrup and process until very smooth (this might take a few minutes). Cover and chill in the refrigerator for at least 2 hours. Then freeze in an ice-cream maker according to the manufacturer's directions.

This attractive, green ice cream looks as good as it tastes. Look for raw pistachios at a natural food store or farmers' market.

pistachio ICE CREAM

1 cup shelled raw pistachios

1 (14-ounce) can full-fat coconut milk

1¼ cups soymilk or other nondairy milk

½ cup granulated sugar or agave syrup

Place the pistachios in a blender and grind them into a fine powder. (It's okay if they start to clump up.) Add the coconut milk, soymilk, and sugar to the blender and process until smooth. Cover and chill in the refrigerator for at least 2 hours. Then freeze in an ice-cream maker according to the manufacturer's directions.

Be sure to allow time for the base to soak up the coconut flavor. Our favorite Thai restaurant serves coconut ice cream garnished with salted peanuts—a delicious combination you might want to try.

coconut ICE CREAM

½ cup unsweetened shredded dried coconut

1 (14-ounce) can full-fat coconut milk

1¼ cups soymilk or other nondairy milk

½ cup granulated sugar or agave syrup

1 teaspoon vanilla extract

Place the shredded coconut in a saucepan on medium-low heat. Stir until the coconut begins to turn slightly golden. Add the coconut milk, soymilk, and sugar and stir to mix. Warm on medium heat until the sugar is dissolved. Remove from the heat and stir in the vanilla extract. Cool to room temperature. Then cover and chill in the refrigerator for 8 to 12 hours.

When you are ready to make the ice cream, pour the base through a fine-mesh strainer placed over a medium bowl. Transfer the strained coconut to a small bowl, cover, and refrigerate; it will be added later.

Freeze the ice-cream base in an ice-cream maker according to the manufacturer's directions. About 5 minutes before the end of the freezing time, when the ice cream is almost to the firmness you desire, add the reserved coconut. Process for 5 more minutes, or until the ice cream reaches the desired consistency.

This is sweet and spicy—perfect after an Asian stir-fry. It's delicious topped with any of the fruit sauces in this book.

ginger ICE CREAM

1¼ cups soymilk or other nondairy milk

⅓ cup peeled and minced fresh ginger

1 (14-ounce) can full-fat coconut milk

½ cup granulated sugar or agave syrup

3 to 4 tablespoons minced crystallized ginger

Pour the soymilk into a small saucepan. Add the fresh ginger and warm on medium-low heat, stirring occasionally, until the soymilk just begins to boil. Cover and remove from the heat. Let steep for 30 minutes.

Place a fine-mesh strainer over a medium bowl. Pour the soymilk mixture through the strainer to remove the ginger. Whisk the coconut milk and sugar into the soymilk. Cover and chill in the refrigerator for at least 3 hours. Then freeze in an ice-cream maker according to the manufacturer's directions.

About 5 minutes before the end of the freezing time, when the ice cream is almost to the firmness you desire, add the crystallized ginger. Process for 5 more minutes, or until the ice cream reaches the desired consistency.

I don't know why cardamom is such an underused spice; I love its exotic flavor. Cardamom goes exceptionally well with lemon, as in the variation that follows.

cardamom ICE CREAM

MAKES 1 QUART

15 cardamom pods

1¼ cups soymilk or other nondairy milk

1 (14-ounce) can full-fat coconut milk

¾ cup granulated sugar or agave syrup

Break open the cardamom pods using a mortar and pestle or the back of a wooden spoon. Release the seeds into a small saucepan and discard the pods. Add the soymilk and warm on medium-low heat, stirring occasionally, until it just begins to boil. Cover and remove from the heat. Let steep for 20 to 30 minutes.

Place a fine-mesh strainer over a medium bowl. Pour the soymilk mixture through the strainer to remove the cardamom seeds. Whisk in the coconut milk and sugar. Cover and chill in the refrigerator for at least 3 hours. Then freeze in an ice-cream maker according to the manufacturer's directions.

lemon-cardamom ice cream: Whisk 5 tablespoons of freshly squeezed lemon juice into the chilled ice-cream base. Freeze as directed.

I love cinnamon in everything from oatmeal to baked goods, so of course I had to try it in ice cream. This tastes great with a slice of apple pie or a warm brownie.

cinnamon ICE CREAM

MAKES 1 QUART

1¼ cups soymilk or other nondairy milk

2 (3-inch) cinnamon sticks

1 (14-ounce) can full-fat coconut milk

½ cup granulated sugar or agave syrup

¼ teaspoon ground cinnamon

Pour the soymilk into a small saucepan. Add the cinnamon sticks and warm on medium-low heat, stirring occasionally, until the soymilk just begins to boil. Cover and remove from the heat. Steep for 30 minutes. Then remove the cinnamon sticks from the soymilk.

Place the coconut milk and sugar in a medium bowl and whisk together. Add the warm soymilk and the ground cinnamon and whisk until well combined. Cover and chill in the refrigerator for at least 3 hours. Then freeze in an ice-cream maker according to the manufacturer's directions.

A hint of rosemary gives this ice cream a wonderful depth of flavor. It's excellent with a fruit pie or crisp.

rosemary ICE CREAM

1¼ cups soymilk or other nondairy milk

4 large sprigs fresh rosemary

1 (14-ounce) **can full-fat coconut milk**

½ cup granulated sugar or agave syrup

Pour the soymilk into a small saucepan and warm on medium-low heat until it just begins to boil. Add the rosemary sprigs, cover, and remove from the heat. Steep for 20 minutes.

Place a fine-mesh strainer over a medium bowl. Pour the soymilk through the strainer to remove the rosemary. Whisk in the coconut milk and sugar. Cover and chill in the refrigerator for at least 3 hours. Then freeze in an ice-cream maker according to the manufacturer's directions.

You can cook a fresh pumpkin for this recipe if you like, but canned works just fine. You can also substitute puréed sweet potato or squash for the pumpkin. Try this ice cream topped with Whipped Orange-Cashew Cream (p. 124).

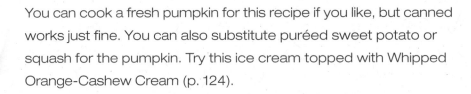

pumpkin spice ICE CREAM

MAKES 1 GENEROUS QUART

1 (14-ounce) can full-fat coconut milk

1 cup puréed cooked pumpkin

½ cup soymilk or other nondairy milk

½ cup maple syrup

1½ teaspoons ground cinnamon

1 teaspoon vanilla extract

½ teaspoon ground nutmeg

¼ teaspoon ground ginger

Combine all of the ingredients in a blender and process until smooth. Cover and chill in the refrigerator for at least 2 hours. Then freeze in an ice-cream maker according to the manufacturer's directions.

This ice cream has a sweet taste with just a bite of spiciness. It's especially great in Mango-Lemongrass Terrine with Lime Syrup (p. 87).

lemongrass ICE CREAM

MAKES 1 QUART

1¼ cups soymilk or other nondairy milk

¼ cup dried lemongrass

1 (14-ounce) can full-fat coconut milk

½ cup granulated sugar or agave syrup

Pour the soymilk into a small saucepan and warm on medium-low heat until it just begins to boil. Stir in the lemongrass. Cover and remove from the heat. Steep for 30 minutes.

Place a fine-mesh strainer over a medium bowl. Pour the soymilk through the strainer to remove the lemongrass. Whisk in the coconut milk and sugar. Cover and chill in the refrigerator for at least 3 hours. Then freeze in an ice-cream maker according to the manufacturer's directions.

Lavender blossoms give this ice cream a unique, delicate flavor. I love it with a mild-flavored cake like pound cake. It's also delicious topped with berries. This is one of my most-requested recipes.

lavender ICE CREAM

MAKES 1 QUART

1¼ cups soymilk or other nondairy milk

¼ cup fresh lavender flowers and buds (about 8 large sprigs)

1 (14-ounce) can full-fat coconut milk

½ cup granulated sugar or agave syrup

Pour the soymilk into a small saucepan and warm on medium-low heat until it just begins to boil. Stir in the lavender flowers and buds. Cover and remove from the heat. Steep for 20 minutes.

Place a fine-mesh strainer over a medium bowl. Pour the soymilk through the strainer to remove the lavender. Whisk in the coconut milk and sugar. Cover and chill in the refrigerator for at least 3 hours. Then freeze in an ice-cream maker according to the manufacturer's directions.

Chai is a spicy Indian tea that has become quite popular in the last few years. I took the same flavors and created this ice cream. Try it after an Indian meal of dal (seasoned lentils) and naan (bread).

chai ICE CREAM

MAKES 1 QUART

1¼ cups soymilk or other nondairy milk

1 teaspoon ground cinnamon

½ teaspoon ground cardamom

10 whole cloves

1 (14-ounce) can full-fat coconut milk

½ cup granulated sugar or agave syrup

1 teaspoon vanilla extract

Pour the soymilk into a small saucepan and add the cinnamon, cardamom, and cloves. Warm on medium-low heat, whisking occasionally, until the soymilk just begins to boil. Cover and remove from the heat. Steep for 15 minutes.

Use a slotted spoon to remove the cloves from the soymilk. Whisk in the coconut milk, sugar, and vanilla extract. Cover and chill in the refrigerator for at least 3 hours. Then freeze in an ice-cream maker according to the manufacturer's directions.

This ice cream combines creamy, rich chocolate with hints of Indian spices. I like this flavor on its own so I can appreciate all the subtle nuances.

chocolate-chai ICE CREAM

MAKES 1 GENEROUS QUART

1¼ cups soymilk or other nondairy milk

1 teaspoon ground cinnamon

10 whole cloves

½ teaspoon ground cardamom

2 ounces unsweetened chocolate

1 (14-ounce) can full-fat coconut milk

½ cup granulated sugar or agave syrup

3 tablespoons cocoa powder

1 teaspoon vanilla extract

Pour the soymilk into a small saucepan and add the cinnamon, cloves, and cardamom. Warm on medium-low heat, whisking occasionally, until the soymilk just begins to boil. Cover and remove from the heat. Steep for 15 minutes.

Use a slotted spoon to remove the cloves. Add the chocolate and stir until it is melted. (You may need to reheat the soymilk on low heat if it is not hot enough to melt the chocolate.) Whisk in the coconut milk, sugar, cocoa powder, and vanilla extract. Cover and chill in the refrigerator for at least 3 hours. Then freeze in an ice-cream maker according to the manufacturer's directions.

This popular Japanese dessert would be perfect after a dinner of miso soup and vegetarian sushi. Look for green tea powder, known as *matcha*, at natural food stores and Asian markets, or order it online.

green tea ICE CREAM

MAKES 1 QUART

1¼ cups soymilk or other nondairy milk

3 tablespoons green tea powder

1 (14-ounce) can full-fat coconut milk

½ cup granulated sugar or agave syrup

Pour the soymilk into a small saucepan. Add the green tea powder and whisk until well combined. Warm on medium-low heat until the soymilk just begins to boil. Cover and remove from the heat. Steep for 15 minutes.

Whisk in the coconut milk and sugar. Cover and chill in the refrigerator for at least 3 hours. Then freeze in an ice-cream maker according to the manufacturer's directions.

fresh and fruity

FRUIT ICE CREAMS AND SHERBETS

2

This section is packed with fruity ice creams and sherbets. The quality of the fruit you use will make a big difference in the quality of the finished product. I like to use locally grown fruit that is cultivated for flavor rather than a long shelf life. I also recommend organic or pesticide-free varieties, as fruit is often heavily sprayed. Summer is the obvious time to make these ice creams, but it's a great idea to buy extra fruit when it's in season to freeze for later use. With frozen fruit, you can make these delicious ice creams year-round; in addition, you can skip the chilling step and freeze the ice cream right away.

Strawberries are abundant where we live on the central coast of California, so this is a flavor we make often. It's best with really red, ripe berries.

strawberry ICE CREAM

MAKES 1 QUART

2½ cups halved strawberries

1 (14-ounce) can full-fat coconut milk

½ cup granulated sugar or agave syrup

2 teaspoons vanilla extract

Combine all of the ingredients in a blender and process until smooth. Cover and chill in the refrigerator for at least 2 hours. Then freeze in an ice-cream maker according to the manufacturer's directions.

This is a terrific flavor for birthday parties or any gathering where there are kids.

strawberry-banana ICE CREAM

MAKES 1 GENEROUS QUART

2 cups sliced strawberries

2 medium bananas

1 (14-ounce) can full-fat coconut milk

½ cup granulated sugar or agave syrup

2 tablespoons freshly squeezed lemon juice

Combine all of the ingredients in a blender and process until smooth. Cover and chill in the refrigerator for at least 2 hours. Then freeze in an ice-cream maker according to the manufacturer's directions.

mango-banana ice cream: Replace the strawberries with 2 cups of diced mango.

This is delicious with either fresh or frozen cherries. The bonus to using frozen cherries is that they're already pitted.

cherry ICE CREAM

MAKES 1 QUART

2 cups pitted dark cherries

1 (14-ounce) can full-fat coconut milk

1/3 to 1/2 cup granulated sugar or agave syrup

1 teaspoon vanilla extract

Combine all of the ingredients in a blender, starting with the smaller amount of sugar, and process until smooth. Taste and add additional sugar, if necessary. Cover and chill in the refrigerator for at least 2 hours. Then freeze in an ice-cream maker according to the manufacturer's directions.

cherry-chocolate chip ice cream: About 5 minutes before the end of the freezing time, when the ice cream is almost to the firmness you desire, add 1/2 cup of mini dark or semisweet chocolate chips or chopped chocolate. Process for 5 more minutes, or until the ice cream reaches the desired consistency.

Blueberries are my favorite berry, so I thought I might be biased about this flavor. It turns out it wasn't just me; it was a favorite of the testers as well.

blueberry ICE CREAM

MAKES 1 QUART

2 cups blueberries

1 (14-ounce) can full-fat coconut milk

½ cup soymilk or other nondairy milk

½ cup granulated sugar or agave syrup

1 teaspoon vanilla extract

Combine all of the ingredients in a blender and process until smooth. Cover and chill in the refrigerator for at least 2 hours. Then freeze in an ice-cream maker according to the manufacturer's directions.

I thought my original Blueberry Ice Cream couldn't get any better, but this flavor proved me wrong! This recipe is actually worth growing fresh lavender for—but if it's not in your garden, look for it at a farmers' market or natural food store.

lavender-blueberry ICE CREAM

MAKES 1 QUART

½ cup soymilk or other nondairy milk

2 tablespoons fresh lavender flowers and buds (about 4 large sprigs)

2 cups blueberries

1 (14-ounce) can full-fat coconut milk

½ cup granulated sugar or agave syrup

1 teaspoon vanilla extract

Pour the soymilk into a small saucepan and warm it on medium-low heat until it just begins to boil. Stir in the lavender flowers and buds. Cover and remove from the heat. Steep for 20 minutes.

Place a fine-mesh strainer over a blender jar. Pour the soymilk mixture through the strainer to remove the lavender. Add the blueberries, coconut milk, sugar, and vanilla extract to the blender and process until smooth. Cover and chill in the refrigerator for at least 3 hours. Then freeze in an ice-cream maker according to the manufacturer's directions.

This beautiful, fuchsia ice cream is made with our favorite summer berries.

triple berry ICE CREAM

MAKES 1 GENEROUS QUART

1 (14-ounce) can
full-fat coconut milk

1 cup sliced strawberries

1 cup blueberries

1 cup raspberries

⅔ cup granulated sugar
or agave syrup

Combine all of the ingredients in a blender and process until smooth. Cover and chill in the refrigerator for at least 2 hours. Then freeze in an ice-cream maker according to the manufacturer's directions.

Some blackberries are sweeter than others. If the berries are very tart, use the larger amount of sweetener.

blackberry ICE CREAM

MAKES 1 GENEROUS QUART

3 cups blackberries

1 (14-ounce) can
full-fat coconut milk

⅔ to ¾ cup granulated
sugar or agave syrup

Combine all of the ingredients in a blender, starting with the smaller amount of sugar, and process until smooth. Taste and add additional sugar, if necessary. Place a fine-mesh strainer over a medium bowl and press the mixture through it to remove the seeds. Cover and chill in the refrigerator for at least 2 hours. Then freeze in an ice-cream maker according to the manufacturer's directions.

This combination came about as a result of a series of coincidences. A friend had given me a bunch of very ripe plums, which needed to be eaten immediately. That same day, on my way home from the farmers' market, I accidentally crushed a half pint of blackberries, so those needed to be used right away as well. Neither fruit was enough for a batch of ice cream on its own, but together—just right. And what a great combination it turned out to be.

blackberry-plum ICE CREAM

MAKES 1 GENEROUS QUART

1 (14-ounce) can full-fat coconut milk

1¼ cups blackberries

1 cup peeled and chopped ripe plums

⅔ cup granulated sugar or agave syrup

Combine all of the ingredients in a blender and process until smooth. If desired, push the mixture through a fine-mesh strainer to remove the blackberry seeds. Cover and chill in the refrigerator for at least 2 hours. Then freeze in an ice-cream maker according to the manufacturer's directions.

If the plums are very ripe, the skins will just slip off as you dice them. I find it easiest to hold each plum over a bowl and chop it right off the pit, so I don't lose any of the juice. This ice cream is a bit messy to make but definitely worth it.

plum ICE CREAM

MAKES 1 GENEROUS QUART

2 cups peeled and chopped ripe plums

1 (14-ounce) can full-fat coconut milk

⅔ cup granulated sugar or agave syrup

Combine all of the ingredients in a blender and process until smooth. Cover and chill in the refrigerator for at least 2 hours. Then freeze in an ice-cream maker according to the manufacturer's directions.

You can skip cooking the peaches if you want to, but a quick simmer really intensifies the peach taste. I start the peaches cooking and then gather the remaining ingredients. By the time I've gotten all of the items together and poured them into the blender, the peaches are ready. I do confess that I usually don't bother peeling the peaches. You don't need to either, if you don't mind a bit of peel now and then.

peach ICE CREAM

MAKES 1½ QUARTS

4 cups peeled and sliced peaches

¼ cup water

1 (14-ounce) can full-fat coconut milk

½ cup granulated sugar or agave syrup

1 teaspoon vanilla extract

Place the peaches and water in a saucepan and bring to a boil on medium-low heat. Reduce the heat to low, cover, and simmer for 5 to 8 minutes, until the peaches soften.

Combine the coconut milk, sugar, and vanilla extract in a blender. Pour in the peaches and process until smooth. Cover and chill in the refrigerator for at least 3 hours. Then freeze in an ice-cream maker according to the manufacturer's directions.

The cashews in this recipe give the ice cream its creaminess instead of coconut milk. Use really ripe, juicy peaches for the best taste. I don't usually bother peeling the peaches unless the skins are really thick or unattractive. In that case, I just pull them off as I dice.

peach-cashew ICE CREAM

MAKES 1 QUART

1 cup raw cashews

3 cups diced peaches

½ cup maple syrup or agave syrup

1 teaspoon vanilla extract

Dash cardamom (optional)

Place the cashews in a blender and grind them into a fine powder. Add the peaches, maple syrup, vanilla extract, and optional cardamom and process until completely smooth (this could take up to 1 to 2 minutes). Chill in the refrigerator for at least 2 hours. Then freeze in an ice-cream maker according to the manufacturer's directions.

I had never heard of apricot ice cream and wasn't sure that it would even work; but I love apricots, so I figured why not try it. And wow! It was amazing. Use ripe, sweet apricots—tree-ripened if possible.

apricot ICE CREAM

MAKES 1½ QUARTS

4½ cups sliced apricots

¼ cup water

1 (14-ounce) can full-fat coconut milk

½ cup granulated sugar

2 teaspoons freshly squeezed lemon juice

⅛ teaspoon almond extract

Place the apricots and water in a saucepan and bring to a boil on medium-low heat. Reduce the heat to low, cover, and simmer for 5 minutes, until the apricots soften.

Combine the coconut milk, sugar, lemon juice, and almond extract in a blender. Pour in the apricots and process until smooth. Cover and chill in the refrigerator for at least 3 hours. Then freeze in an ice-cream maker according to the manufacturer's directions.

peach-apricot ice cream: Reduce the amount of apricots to 2½ cups and add 2 cups of peeled and sliced peaches.

If you find orange sherbet too strong, try this creamier, less intensely flavored ice cream. If you include the optional liqueur, you will need to harden this in the freezer for a few hours.

orange ICE CREAM

MAKES 1 GENEROUS QUART

2 cups freshly squeezed orange juice

1 (14-ounce) can full-fat coconut milk

⅓ cup granulated sugar or agave syrup

2 tablespoons Grand Marnier or Triple Sec (optional)

Combine all of the ingredients in a medium bowl and whisk until well combined. Cover and chill in the refrigerator for at least 2 hours. Then freeze in an ice-cream maker according to the manufacturer's directions.

This is a very different and delicious ice cream. Adjust the amount of marmalade to suit your taste and try using other marmalades besides orange. A vendor at my local farmers' market sells all kinds of interesting citrus blends. We especially like this ice cream with her lemon-nectarine marmalade.

orange marmalade ICE CREAM

MAKES 1 QUART

1 (14-ounce) can full-fat coconut milk

1 cup soymilk or other nondairy milk

¾ to 1 cup orange marmalade

Place all of the ingredients in a medium bowl and whisk until well combined. Cover and chill in the refrigerator for at least 2 hours. Then freeze in an ice-cream maker according to the manufacturer's directions.

This is slightly milder and creamier than Lemon Sorbet (p. 62). It's wonderful topped with fresh berries.

lemon ICE CREAM

1 (14-ounce) can full-fat coconut milk

1 cup soymilk or other nondairy milk

¾ cup granulated sugar or agave syrup

5 tablespoons freshly squeezed lemon juice

Place the coconut milk, soymilk, and sugar in a medium bowl and whisk until well combined. Cover and chill in the refrigerator for at least 2 hours. Then whisk in the lemon juice and freeze in an ice-cream maker according to the manufacturer's directions.

This is a lovely, creamy, slightly tart ice cream.

lime ICE CREAM

1 (14-ounce) can full-fat coconut milk

1 cup soymilk or other nondairy milk

⅔ cup granulated sugar or agave syrup

6 tablespoons freshly squeezed lime juice

Place the coconut milk, soymilk, and sugar in a medium bowl and whisk until well combined. Cover and chill in the refrigerator for at least 2 hours. Then whisk in the lime juice and freeze in an ice-cream maker according to the manufacturer's directions.

If you like cheesecake, you'll love this ice cream. Try it topped with Fresh Raspberry Sauce (p. 121) or Mango Sauce (p. 122).

lemon cheesecake ICE CREAM

MAKES 1 QUART

1 large lemon

1 (12-ounce) package firm silken tofu

8 ounces nondairy cream cheese

⅔ cup agave syrup

½ cup soymilk or other nondairy milk

2 teaspoons vanilla extract

Finely grate the peel from the lemon, taking care to get only the yellow portion, not the bitter white pith. Put the grated peel in a small bowl in the refrigerator for later use.

Cut the lemon in half and extract the juice (you should have about 4 tablespoons of juice). Transfer the lemon juice to a food processor or blender and add the tofu, nondairy cream cheese, agave syrup, soymilk, and vanilla extract. Process until smooth. Cover and chill in the refrigerator for at least 2 hours. Then freeze in an ice-cream maker according to the manufacturer's directions.

About 5 minutes before the end of the freezing time, when the ice cream is almost to the firmness you desire, add the lemon peel. Process for 5 more minutes, or until the ice cream reaches the desired consistency.

This beautiful, brightly colored sherbet is so creamy and delicious. If you use frozen raspberries, thaw them first or it will be difficult to strain out the seeds.

red raspberry SHERBET

MAKES 1 GENEROUS QUART

4 cups raspberries

1 (14-ounce) can full-fat coconut milk

¾ cup granulated sugar or agave syrup

1 teaspoon vanilla extract

Combine all of the ingredients in a blender and process until smooth. Place a fine-mesh strainer over a medium bowl, pour the blended mixture into the strainer, and press it through to remove the seeds. Cover and chill in the refrigerator for at least 2 hours. Then freeze in an ice-cream maker according to the manufacturer's directions.

This sherbet is very tart. It goes well with a sweet dessert, like a fruit tart or poppy seed cake.

lemon-lime SHERBET

MAKES 1 QUART

1 (14-ounce) can full-fat coconut milk

1 cup agave syrup

Juice of 2 lemons

Juice of 2 limes

Place all of the ingredients in a medium bowl and whisk until well combined. Cover and chill in the refrigerator for at least 2 hours. Then freeze in an ice-cream maker according to the manufacturer's directions.

NOTE: This sherbet is fairly soft, so you will need to harden it in the freezer for a few hours before serving.

You might think I should have put orange sherbet as the main recipe and tangerine as the variation, but I just love tangerines. Of course that's just me—the orange is delicious too. You'll have to decide which is your favorite.

tangerine SHERBET

MAKES ABOUT 1 QUART

1 (14-ounce) **can full-fat coconut milk** (cream only)

2¼ cups tangerine juice, chilled

¼ cup granulated sugar or agave syrup

Open the can of coconut milk and carefully scoop out the hard white cream on top. Discard the liquid. Place the coconut cream in a medium bowl. Add the juice and sugar and whisk until well combined. Cover and chill in the refrigerator for at least 2 hours (see note). Then freeze in an ice-cream maker according to the manufacturer's directions.

orange sherbet: Use 2¼ cups of orange juice instead of the tangerine juice.

NOTE: It is not essential to chill this base because it should be fairly cold from the juice, but chilling it will give you a harder sherbet straight from the ice-cream maker.

Pineapple is so naturally sweet that you don't need to use much sweetener to make this tropical sherbet.

pineapple SHERBET

MAKES 1 GENEROUS QUART

1 (15-ounce) **can crushed pineapple, or 2 cups fresh pineapple purée**

1 (14-ounce) **can full-fat coconut milk**

⅓ **cup granulated sugar** lor **agave syrup**

2 **tablespoons freshly squeezed lemon juice**

Combine all of the ingredients in a blender and process until smooth. Cover and chill in the refrigerator for at least 2 hours. Then freeze in an ice-cream maker according to the manufacturer's directions.

piña colada sherbet: After chilling the ice-cream base in the refrigerator, whisk in ¼ cup of light rum. Freeze as directed. The sherbet will be fairly soft, so you'll need to harden it for a few hours in the freezer before serving.

the lighter side

LOW-FAT ICE CREAMS, FROZEN YOGURTS, AND SORBETS

3

Looking for something a little lighter? Not only are these frozen treats easy on your waistline, they are full of nutritious ingredients like tofu, yogurt, and fruit. Though these ice creams, frozen yogurts, and sorbets have fewer calories than the full-fat ice creams, they have plenty of flavor. Your friends and family will never know they are eating something healthful!

Fruit and silken tofu make these low-fat ice creams thick and creamy without the fat and calories of coconut milk. My family loves these flavors; they don't even know they are eating something low fat. And don't worry if someone doesn't like tofu; no one will be able to tell it's in the ice cream. If you use frozen fruit in these recipes, you will need to thaw it a bit or it will be difficult to blend the bases.

I serve this flavor frequently to family and guests, and no one has ever suspected that it's low in fat.

low-fat strawberry ICE CREAM

MAKES 1 GENEROUS QUART

2½ cups halved strawberries

1 (12-ounce) package silken tofu

½ cup soymilk or other nondairy milk

½ cup granulated sugar or agave syrup

2 tablespoons freshly squeezed lemon juice

1 tablespoon vanilla extract

Combine all of the ingredients in a blender and process until smooth and uniformly pink. Cover and chill in the refrigerator for at least 2 hours. Then freeze in an ice-cream maker according to the manufacturer's directions.

low-fat blueberry ice cream: Replace the strawberries with 2 cups of blueberries.

Whether low fat or full fat, strawberry-banana is a flavor kids love.

low-fat strawberry-banana ICE CREAM

MAKES 1 GENEROUS QUART

2 cups halved strawberries

2 bananas, peeled and sliced

1 (12-ounce) package silken tofu

½ cup soymilk or other nondairy milk

¼ cup granulated sugar or agave syrup

1 teaspoon vanilla extract

Combine all of the ingredients in a blender and process until smooth. Cover and chill in the refrigerator for at least 2 hours. Then freeze in an ice-cream maker according to the manufacturer's directions.

This tastes a lot like eggnog. It's perfect for the holidays with pumpkin or apple pie.

low-fat banana-nog ICE CREAM

MAKES 1 QUART

1¾ cups soymilk or other nondairy milk

1 (12-ounce) package silken tofu

½ cup agave syrup or maple syrup

1 banana

3 tablespoons rum or brandy (optional)

2 teaspoons vanilla extract

1 teaspoon ground cinnamon

¼ teaspoon ground nutmeg

Combine all of the ingredients in a blender and process until smooth. Cover and chill in the refrigerator for at least 2 hours. Then freeze in an ice-cream maker according to the manufacturer's directions.

NOTE: If you include the rum or brandy, this ice cream will be on the soft side, so you will need to harden it in the freezer for a few hours. This will also give the flavor time to develop.

If you're using frozen raspberries, thaw them completely before making this ice cream. Not only is this flavor hard to blend with frozen fruit, it's almost impossible to strain out the seeds.

low-fat raspberry ICE CREAM

MAKES 1 GENEROUS QUART

3 cups raspberries

1 cup soymilk or other nondairy milk

1 (12-ounce) package silken tofu

½ cup granulated sugar or agave syrup

1 teaspoon vanilla extract

Combine the raspberries and soymilk in a blender and process until smooth. Place a fine-mesh strainer over a bowl, pour the blended mixture into the strainer, and press it through to remove the seeds. Pour the strained mixture back into the blender. Add the tofu, sugar, and vanilla extract and process until smooth and uniformly pink. Cover and chill in the refrigerator for at least 2 hours. Then freeze in an ice-cream maker according to the manufacturer's directions.

I make this with fresh pineapple when I can, but frozen or canned pineapple works just fine as well.

low-fat pineapple ICE CREAM

MAKES 1 GENEROUS QUART

3 cups pineapple chunks

1 (12-ounce) package silken tofu

¾ cup soymilk or other nondairy milk

½ cup granulated sugar or agave syrup

1 teaspoon vanilla extract

½ cup cold minced pineapple (optional)

Combine the pineapple chunks, tofu, soymilk, sugar, and vanilla extract in a blender and process until smooth. Cover and chill in the refrigerator for at least 2 hours. Then freeze in an ice-cream maker according to the manufacturer's directions.

About 5 minutes before the end of the freezing time, when the ice cream is almost to the firmness you desire, add the optional minced pineapple. Process for 5 more minutes, or until the ice cream reaches the desired consistency.

Look for nondairy yogurts made from soy or rice at a well-stocked supermarket or natural food store. Frozen yogurt is quick to make and, as long as all of the ingredients are cold, no advance chilling is needed. Just as the sweetness of fruits can vary, so can the sweetness of yogurts. Taste the base before adding the sweetener to see if you need it. Of course, if the base is not sweet enough when using the amount of sweetener called for in the recipe, add additional sweetener to taste.

frozen yogurts

I like to buy extra strawberries in the summer, when they're in season, and freeze them so I can make this all year round. Just be sure to thaw frozen strawberries or the base will be too difficult to blend.

strawberry FROZEN YOGURT

MAKES 1 QUART

2½ cups strawberry nondairy yogurt

2 cups halved strawberries

2 tablespoons granulated sugar or agave syrup, if needed

Combine the yogurt and strawberries in a blender and process until smooth. Sweeten with the sugar to taste, if needed. If the mixture is cold, it may be frozen immediately; otherwise, chill it in the refrigerator for at least 2 hours. Freeze in an ice-cream maker according to the manufacturer's directions.

NOTE: If the strawberries are very sweet, omit the sweetener. With fresh, ripe strawberries, I usually don't need it; but sometimes with frozen strawberries, or those at the start of the season, I do.

This flavor is tangy and full of vanilla flavor. It's an excellent accompaniment to a sweet dessert.

vanilla FROZEN YOGURT

1 (27-ounce) container vanilla nondairy yogurt (2½ cups)

1 cup soymilk or nondairy milk

½ cup soy creamer or full-fat coconut milk

¼ cup granulated sugar or agave syrup, or to taste

1 tablespoon vanilla extract

Place all of the ingredients in a large bowl and whisk until well combined. If the mixture is cold, it may be frozen immediately; otherwise, chill it in the refrigerator for at least 2 hours. Freeze in an ice-cream maker according to the manufacturer's directions.

This is especially good with Lemon Sauce (p. 121).

blueberry FROZEN YOGURT

2 cups blueberries

2 cups vanilla nondairy yogurt

2 tablespoons granulated sugar or agave syrup

2 tablespoons freshly squeezed lemon juice

Combine all of the ingredients in a blender and process until smooth. If the mixture is cold, it may be frozen immediately; otherwise, chill it in the refrigerator for at least 2 hours. Freeze in an ice-cream maker according to the manufacturer's directions.

I like to serve this with Coconut Cream Sauce (p. 123). Frozen or canned pineapple can be used if you don't have a fresh one.

pineapple FROZEN YOGURT

MAKES 1 QUART

2½ cups pineapple chunks

1½ cups vanilla or
pineapple nondairy yogurt

Combine the pineapple and yogurt in a blender and process until smooth. If the mixture is cold, it may be frozen immediately; otherwise, chill it in the refrigerator for at least 2 hours. Freeze in an ice-cream maker according to the manufacturer's directions.

Use ripe, juicy peaches and the peel will slip right off as you slice them.

peach FROZEN YOGURT

MAKES 1 QUART

2 cups vanilla or peach
nondairy yogurt

2 cups peeled and
diced peaches

2 tablespoons granulated
sugar or agave syrup,
if needed

Combine the yogurt and peaches in a blender and process until smooth. Sweeten with the sugar to taste, if needed. If the mixture is cold, it may be frozen immediately; otherwise, chill it in the refrigerator for at least 2 hours. Freeze in an ice-cream maker according to the manufacturer's directions.

banana-peach frozen yogurt: Add 1 large banana along with the peaches.

This is my favorite of the frozen yogurts. Since this flavor is low in fat and sugar, why not try our favorite combination and serve it over a warm, fudgy brownie.

dark cherry FROZEN YOGURT

MAKES 1 QUART

3 cups cherry nondairy yogurt

1¼ cups pitted dark cherries

2 tablespoons freshly squeezed lemon juice

Granulated sugar or agave syrup, if needed

½ cup chopped dark cherries

Combine the yogurt, pitted cherries, and lemon juice in a blender and process until smooth. Sweeten with a little sugar to taste, if needed. If the mixture is cold, it may be frozen immediately; otherwise, chill it in the refrigerator for at least 2 hours. Freeze in an ice-cream maker according to the manufacturer's directions.

About 5 minutes before the end of the freezing time, when the frozen yogurt is just about to the firmness you desire, add the chopped cherries. Process for 5 more minutes, or until the frozen yogurt reaches the desired consistency.

I was never a big fan of sorbet—my experience being the overly sweetened, icy concoctions offered as a dairy-free alternative at ice-cream parlors. But homemade sorbets, made with fresh, ripe fruit, have given me a whole new perspective. These light, refreshing treats, bursting with fruit flavor, with maybe a subtle hint of an herbal infusion or liqueur, have made a sorbet lover out of me. They're perfect as a dessert after a rich meal or as an energizing pick-me-up on a hot summer day.

sorbets

This sorbet looks just like a kiwi, with its bright green color and flecks of black seeds.

kiwi SORBET

MAKES 1 QUART

3 cups peeled and chopped kiwis

½ cup granulated sugar

6 tablespoons freshly squeezed lemon juice

1 cup cold water

¼ cup Limoncello liqueur (optional)

Agave syrup, if needed (see note)

Place the kiwis, sugar, and lemon juice in a small bowl and stir until well combined. Cover and refrigerate for 1 hour.

Pour the kiwi mixture into a blender. Add the water and optional liqueur and process until smooth. Taste and add a little agave syrup if the mixture is not sweet enough. Freeze in an ice-cream maker according to the manufacturer's directions.

NOTE: If you omit the liqueur, you will probably need additional sweetener. If you include the liqueur, the sorbet will need to harden in the freezer for several hours, or until it reaches the desired consistency.

This is like eating orange juice with a spoon.

orange SORBET

MAKES 1 QUART

3½ cups freshly squeezed
orange juice, chilled

3 to 5 tablespoons agave
syrup (depending on the
sweetness of the oranges)

3 tablespoons Triple Sec
or Grand Marnier (optional)

Place all of the ingredients in a medium bowl and whisk until well combined. Freeze in an ice-cream maker according to the manufacturer's directions.

This sorbet just bursts with sweet strawberry flavor. Best of all, it's quick and easy to make.

strawberry SORBET

MAKES 1 GENEROUS QUART

5 cups halved strawberries

½ cup agave syrup

Juice of ½ lemon

Combine all of the ingredients in a blender and process until smooth. If the mixture is cold, it may be frozen immediately; otherwise, chill it in the refrigerator for at least 2 hours. Then freeze in an ice-cream maker according to the manufacturer's directions.

strawberry daiquiri sorbet: Replace the lemon juice with the juice of 1 whole lime and add 2 tablespoons of light rum. Serve it soft, like a slushy, or harden the sorbet in the freezer for a few hours.

I had the most delicious strawberry lemonade at the Santa Barbara Earth Day Festival. It inspired me to create this sorbet.

strawberry lemonade SORBET

MAKES 1 QUART

3 cups halved strawberries

⅔ cup agave syrup

½ cup freshly squeezed lemon juice

½ cup cold water

Combine all of the ingredients in a blender and process until smooth. If the mixture is cold, it may be frozen immediately; otherwise, chill it in the refrigerator for at least 2 hours. Then freeze in an ice-cream maker according to the manufacturer's directions.

My daughters call this frozen lemonade. We especially love it topped with fresh, sweet strawberries or blueberries.

lemon SORBET

MAKES ABOUT 1 QUART

1½ cups granulated sugar

2 cups boiling water

1⅛ cups freshly squeezed lemon juice

Place the sugar in a heatproof bowl. Pour the boiling water over it and whisk until dissolved. Whisk in the lemon juice. Cool slightly. Chill in the refrigerator for about 3 hours, or until cold. Then freeze in an ice-cream maker according to the manufacturer's directions.

lemon daiquiri sorbet: Add 2 tablespoons of light rum to the chilled sorbet base. Freeze as directed. The sorbet will need to be hardened in the freezer for a few hours before serving.

Lime has a unique taste that I love. Try this topped with fresh blueberries.

lime SORBET

MAKES ABOUT 1 QUART

1½ cups granulated sugar

2 cups boiling water

1⅛ cups freshly squeezed lime juice

Place the sugar in a heatproof bowl. Pour the boiling water over it and whisk until dissolved. Whisk in the lime juice. Cool slightly. Chill in the refrigerator for 3 hours, or until cold. Then freeze in an ice-cream maker according to the manufacturer's directions.

Lemon thyme from my garden adds a wonderful flavor to this sorbet. It is excellent served with shortbread cookies. If at all possible, use organic lemons for the juice and peel.

lemon thyme SORBET

MAKES ABOUT 1 QUART

6 medium lemons

2 cups water

1½ cups granulated sugar

¾ cup fresh lemon thyme sprigs

Use a vegetable peeler to peel off strips of the yellow part of the lemon peel. Bring the water to a boil in a small saucepan. Remove from the heat and whisk in the sugar until it dissolves. Add the lemon thyme and lemon peel strips. Cover and steep for 1 hour.

Strain though a fine-mesh strainer to remove the lemon thyme and lemon peel. Cut the lemons in half and use a citrus juicer to extract juice (you should have about 1⅛ cups of juice). Whisk in the lemon juice and chill in the refrigerator for 3 hours, or until cold. Then freeze in an ice-cream maker according to the manufacturer's directions.

Pomegranates have as many antioxidants as red wine and green tea. Paired with nutritious strawberries, this is a treat for your health as well as your taste buds.

pomegranate-strawberry SORBET

MAKES ABOUT 1 QUART

1½ cups unsweetened pomegranate juice

1 cup halved strawberries

½ cup agave syrup

½ cups water

1 tablespoon freshly squeezed lemon juice

Combine all of the ingredients in a blender and process until smooth. If the mixture is cold, it may be frozen immediately; otherwise, chill it in the refrigerator for at least 2 hours. Freeze in an ice-cream maker according to the manufacturer's directions.

This sorbet is a delicious way to introduce rhubarb to those who haven't tried it—or don't even know what it is. It's wonderful served with pound cake.

strawberry-rhubarb SORBET

MAKES 1 QUART

3 cups sliced rhubarb
(½-inch slices)

¼ cup water

1 tablespoon peeled and minced fresh ginger

2 cups halved strawberries

⅔ cup agave syrup

2 tablespoons vodka
(optional)

Combine the rhubarb, water, and ginger in a medium saucepan and bring to a boil. Reduce the heat and simmer for 5 minutes, or until the rhubarb is soft. Cool slightly.

Transfer the rhubarb mixture to a blender. Add the strawberries and agave syrup and process until smooth. Chill in the refrigerator for at least 3 hours. Whisk in the vodka, if using. Then freeze in an ice-cream maker according to the manufacturer's directions.

NOTE: If you include the vodka, the sorbet will need to harden in the freezer for several hours, or until it reaches the desired consistency.

If you include the liqueur, this sorbet will need to be hardened in the freezer for a few hours. Kirsch liqueur can be hard to find; Chambord makes a good substitute.

cherry SORBET

MAKES 1 GENEROUS QUART

3½ cups pitted
dark cherries

¾ cup cold water

⅓ to ½ cup granulated
sugar or agave syrup

2 tablespoons freshly
squeezed lemon juice

2 tablespoons Kirsch
liqueur (optional)

Combine all of the ingredients in a blender, starting with the lesser amount of sugar, and process until smooth. Taste and add additional sugar, if necessary. If the mixture is cold, it may be frozen immediately; otherwise, chill it in the refrigerator for at least 2 hours. Freeze in an ice-cream maker according to the manufacturer's directions.

This is a true treat for apricot lovers. Try to get tree-ripened apricots, if possible.

apricot SORBET

MAKES 1 QUART

3 cups sliced apricots

½ cup granulated sugar
or agave syrup

3 tablespoons freshly
squeezed lemon or
orange juice

1 cup cold water

2 tablespoons Triple Sec
or Grand Marnier (optional)

Combine the apricots, sugar, and lemon juice in a bowl. Cover and refrigerate for 1 hour. Pour the apricot mixture into a blender. Add the water and optional liqueur and process until smooth. Taste and add additional sweetener, if necessary. Freeze in an ice-cream maker according to the manufacturer's directions.

The hardest part about making this sorbet is finding the perfect melon. A ripe cantaloupe will be slightly soft in the stem area and will smell sweet.

cantaloupe SORBET

MAKES 1 QUART

4 cups diced cantaloupe

⅓ cup agave syrup

3 tablespoons freshly squeezed lemon juice

Combine all of the ingredients in a blender and process until smooth. If the mixture is cold, it may be frozen immediately; otherwise, chill it in the refrigerator for at least 1 hour. Freeze in an ice-cream maker according to the manufacturer's directions. Then harden it in the freezer for several hours.

SERVING SUGGESTION:

To impress your family and friends, try this fun serving idea. Cut the melon in half, remove the seeds, and carefully scoop out the flesh while leaving the shell intact. Fill the shells with the frozen sorbet and level off the top with a knife. Scoop out a small hole in the center to look like the seed cavity. Freeze for several hours. When ready to serve, use a large knife to cut the melon into wedges.

honeydew sorbet: Substitute honeydew melon for the cantaloupe.

When I lived in New England there were always wild blueberries to pick along the side of the road in summer. Unfortunately, they're hard to find in California. Though wild blueberries are the most flavorful, any type of blueberry will taste great in this sorbet. I really like lime juice in this sorbet, but lemon juice tastes just fine if you don't have limes on hand.

blueberry SORBET

MAKES 1 GENEROUS QUART

4½ cups blueberries

⅔ cup agave syrup

½ cup water

¼ cup freshly squeezed lime juice

Combine all of the ingredients in a blender and process until smooth. If the mixture is cold, it may be frozen immediately; otherwise, chill it in the refrigerator for at least 2 hours. Freeze in an ice-cream maker according to the manufacturer's directions.

No sweeteners are used in this delicious sorbet—it's all fruit!

blueberry-banana SORBET

MAKES 1 QUART

3 bananas

1 cup blueberries

1 cup unsweetened apple juice

Combine all of the ingredients in a blender and process until smooth. If the mixture is cold, it may be frozen immediately; otherwise, chill it in the refrigerator for at least 2 hours. Freeze in an ice-cream maker according to the manufacturer's directions.

This sorbet is sweet and creamy—more like ice cream than sorbet.

mango SORBET

MAKES 1 QUART

3 cups peeled and diced mango

Juice of 1 lemon

1 cup cold water

⅓ cup granulated sugar or agave syrup

Combine the mango and lemon juice in a small bowl. Cover and refrigerate for 1 hour. Pour the mango mixture into a blender, add the water and sugar, and process until smooth. Taste and add additional sugar, if necessary. Freeze in an ice-cream maker according to the manufacturer's directions.

Since I like red wine with a hint of raspberries, I thought I'd try raspberries with a hint of wine. Don't worry if you don't have any wine on hand; this sorbet is wonderful without it as well.

raspberry SORBET

MAKES 1 GENEROUS QUART

5 cups raspberries

¾ cup agave syrup

½ cup water

Juice of ½ lemon

¼ cup fruity red wine, like Syrah (optional)

Combine the raspberries, agave syrup, water, and lemon juice in a blender and process until smooth. Place a fine-mesh strainer over a medium bowl, pour the blended mixture into the strainer, and press it through to remove the seeds. Chill in the refrigerator for at least 2 hours, or until cold. Whisk in the wine, if using. Then freeze in an ice-cream maker according to the manufacturer's directions.

NOTE: If you include the wine, the sorbet will need to harden in the freezer for several hours, or until it reaches the desired consistency.

This is a tasty combination of tart and sweet flavors. To make this sorbet super easy, use frozen mango chunks (thawed slightly) and store-bought tangerine juice. If you can't find tangerine juice, orange juice will work fine too.

tango-mango SORBET

MAKES ABOUT 1 QUART

3 cups peeled and diced mango

1¼ cups freshly squeezed tangerine juice, chilled

¼ cup granulated sugar or agave syrup

Combine all of the ingredients in a blender and process until smooth. Freeze in an ice-cream maker according to the manufacturer's directions.

This is a very flavorful and beautifully colored sorbet. For a striking presentation, serve it in champagne glasses and garnish it with orange slices.

cranberry-orange SORBET

MAKES 1 GENEROUS QUART

2⅔ cups unsweetened cranberry juice, chilled

1¼ cups agave syrup

⅔ cup freshly squeezed orange juice

Finely grated peel of 1 orange

Place the cranberry juice, agave syrup, and orange juice in a medium bowl and whisk until well combined. Freeze in an ice-cream maker according to the manufacturer's directions.

About 5 minutes before the end of the freezing time, when the sorbet is almost to the firmness you desire, add the orange peel. Process for 5 more minutes.

NOTE: This sorbet is fairly soft, so you will need to harden it in the freezer for a few hours before serving.

This sorbet bursts with apples and spices. It's a bit like frozen mulled cider.

spiced apple SORBET

MAKES 1 QUART

2½ cups unsweetened apple juice

2 (3-inch) cinnamon sticks

3 cardamom pods

6 whole cloves

1½ cups unsweetened applesauce

¼ cup maple syrup

2 tablespoons rum or brandy (optional)

Place the apple juice, cinnamon sticks, cardamom pods, and cloves in a medium saucepan. Warm on medium heat until the juice begins to boil. Reduce the heat to low, cover, and simmer for 20 minutes. Remove the spices and whisk in the applesauce, maple syrup, and optional rum. Chill in the refrigerator for at least 3 hours, or until cold. Freeze in an ice-cream maker according to the manufacturer's directions.

NOTE: If you include the rum, the sorbet will need to harden in the freezer for several hours, or until it reaches the desired consistency.

just desserts

PIES, CAKES, TORTES, AND CRUSTS

4

I love making ice-cream pies, cakes, and tortes for my guests.
Not only do they look impressive, they taste great too.
Best of all, they can be made ahead of time.

Ice-cream desserts need to be tempered before they are served for the best taste and ease of slicing. If the dessert is frozen solid, leave it at room temperature for fifteen to twenty minutes or in the refrigerator for forty to sixty minutes. To slice, use a strong, sharp knife dipped in warm water.

pies, cakes, and tortes

Before I stopped eating dairy products, it never even occurred to me that ice-cream pies could be made at home. It turns out they are very easy to make, and it's so much fun coming up with new combinations of ice creams, crusts, and toppings.

basic ice-cream PIE

CRUST

Your favorite cookie crust (see pp. 79–80), **prepared in a 9-inch pie pan**

ICE-CREAM FILLING

1 quart homemade ice cream, frozen yogurt, or sorbet

TOPPINGS TO SPRINKLE
(one or more; optional)

chocolate chips

chopped or sliced nuts

grated citrus peel

shaved chocolate

shredded coconut

sliced fruit or berries

sprinkles

TOPPINGS TO SERVE
(one or more; optional)

sauce

vegan whipped topping

Place the prepared crust in the freezer for 15 minutes. Carefully spread the ice cream evenly into the crust. Sprinkle with the toppings of your choice, if desired. Cover the pie with parchment paper, plastic wrap, or aluminum foil and freeze for at least 3 hours, or until firm. Serve with the sauce or whipped topping of your choice, if desired.

TABLE 2 Specialty ice-cream pies

TYPE OF PIE	CRUST	FILLING	TOPPINGS TO SPRINKLE	TOPPINGS TO SERVE
Chocolate-Coconut-Almond Pie	Chocolate Sandwich Cookie Crust (p. 80)	Coconut Ice Cream (p. 27)	chocolate chips and chopped toasted almonds	—
Chocolate–Peanut Butter Pie	Chocolate–Peanut Butter Sandwich Cookie Crust (p. 80)	Peanut Butter Ice Cream (p. 23)	mini chocolate chips and chopped roasted peanuts	—
Ginger Peach Pie	Ginger Crème Sandwich Cookie Crust (p. 80)	Peach Ice Cream (p. 43)	—	Whipped Tofu Almond Cream (p. 125)
Ginger Pumpkin Pie	Gingersnap Cookie Crust (p. 79)	Pumpkin Spice Ice Cream (p. 32)	—	Whipped Cashew Cream (p. 124)
Grasshopper Pie	Mint Chocolate Sandwich Cookie Crust (p. 80)	Mint Ice Cream (p. 15)	chocolate chips	—
Key Lime Pie	Graham Cracker Crust (p. 79)	Lime Ice Cream (p. 46)	grated lime peel	Whipped Tofu Cream (p. 125)
Lemon Cheesecake Pie	Graham Cracker Crust (p. 79)	Lemon Cheesecake Ice Cream (p. 47)	grated lemon peel	Fresh Raspberry Sauce (p. 121)
Lemon Chiffon Pie	Vanilla Wafer Cookie Crust (p. 79)	Lemon Ice Cream (p. 46)	grated lemon peel	Whipped Tofu Cream (p. 125)
Mud Pie	Chocolate Sandwich Cookie Crust (p. 80)	Coffee Ice Cream (p. 21)	chocolate chips and chopped walnuts	Hot Fudge Sauce (p. 116) and Whipped Tofu Cream (p. 125)
Strawberry Chiffon Pie	Vanilla Wafer Cookie Crust (p. 79)	Strawberry Ice Cream (p. 38)	halved strawberries	Whipped Tofu Cream (p. 125)
Strawberry Lemonade Pie	Lemon Cookie Crust (p. 79)	Strawberry Lemonade Sorbet (p. 62)	—	Fresh Strawberry Sauce (p. 119) and Whipped Tofu Cream (p. 125)
Triple-Chocolate Mousse Pie	Chocolate Sandwich Cookie Crust (p. 80)	Chocolate Mousse Ice Cream (p. 18)	—	Whipped Tofu Chocolate Cream (p. 125)

Ice-cream cakes are perfect for birthday parties and other celebrations, when you want a special dessert that can serve a lot of people.

basic ice-cream CAKE

CAKE

Your favorite sponge cake, baked in a 9-inch springform pan lined with parchment paper for easy removal

ICE-CREAM FILLING

2 quarts homemade ice cream or frozen yogurt

TOPPINGS *(choose one or more; optional)*

chocolate chips

chopped or sliced nuts

sauce

shaved chocolate

shredded coconut

sprinkles

vegan whipped topping

Cool the cake and remove it from the pan. Spread 1 quart of the ice cream evenly in the springform pan. Carefully place the cooled cake on top of the ice cream (don't worry if it breaks or cracks—it won't show). Spread the remaining quart of ice cream evenly over the cake to fill the pan. Cover and freeze for at least 3 hours before serving, or until firm.

When ready to serve, remove the sides of the springform pan and invert the cake onto a serving plate. If you like, spread whipped topping over the cake, drizzle it with sauce, and/or decorate it with other toppings of your choice.

TABLE 3 Specialty ice-cream cakes

TYPE OF CAKE	SPONGE CAKE FLAVOR	FILLING	TOPPING
Black Forest Cake	chocolate	Dark Cherry Frozen Yogurt (p. 59)	Hardening Chocolate Sauce (p. 118)
Chocolate-Almond Cake	almond	Chocolate-Almond Ice Cream (p. 16)	Whipped Tofu Almond Cream (p. 125) and sliced almonds
Chocolate-Raspberry Cake	chocolate	Chocolate-Raspberry Ice Cream (p. 19)	Fresh Raspberry Sauce (p. 121)
Happy Birthday Cake	vanilla	Chocolate Ice Cream (p. 16) and Strawberry Ice Cream (p. 38)	Whipped Tofu Cream (p. 125) and colored sprinkles

This dessert is rich and chocolaty—a wonderful dinner-party dessert.

mocha-almond TORTE

1 Chocolate Cookie Crust
(p. 79), **prepared in a
9-inch springform pan**

1 quart Mocha Ice Cream
(p. 22)

¾ cup dark or semisweet
chocolate chips

2 tablespoons
vegetable oil

1 cup sliced almonds

Whipped Tofu Almond
Cream (p. 125)

Put the crust in the freezer for 15 minutes. Carefully spread the ice cream evenly into the crust. Cover with parchment paper, plastic wrap, or aluminum foil. Freeze for at least 3 hours.

Melt the chocolate chips and oil together in a double boiler over gently simmering water or in a glass bowl in the microwave. Whisk until smooth. Remove the torte from the freezer. Carefully run a knife around the outside of the torte along the edge of the pan. Remove the sides of the pan. Drizzle and spread the melted chocolate over the top of the torte. (It's okay if some drips down the sides.) Immediately sprinkle the almonds over the chocolate. Temper and serve or freeze to serve later. Serve with Whipped Tofu Almond Cream.

This tastes like a frozen candy bar—luscious coconut filling wrapped in dark chocolate.

chocolate-coconut TORTE

MAKES 12 SERVINGS

1 Chocolate Cookie Crust (p. 79), **prepared in a 9-inch springform pan**

1 quart Coconut Ice Cream (p. 27)

¾ cup dark or semisweet chocolate chips

2 tablespoons vegetable oil

⅓ cup unsweetened shredded dried coconut

Put the crust in the freezer for 15 minutes. Carefully spread the ice cream evenly into the crust. Cover with parchment paper, plastic wrap, or aluminum foil. Freeze for at least 3 hours.

Melt the chocolate chips and oil together in a double boiler over gently simmering water or in a glass bowl in the microwave. Whisk until smooth. Remove the torte from the freezer. Carefully run a knife around the outside of the torte along the edge of the pan. Remove the sides of the pan. Drizzle and spread the melted chocolate over the top of the torte. (It's okay if some drips down the sides.) Immediately sprinkle the coconut over the chocolate. Temper and serve or freeze to serve later.

This dessert combines both dark and white chocolate and is delightfully infused with orange flavor.

orange-chocolate TORTE

MAKES 12 SERVINGS

Fudge Brownie Crust
(p. 78), **prepared in a
9-inch round cake pan**

Orange-Chocolate Ice
Cream (p. 17)

White Chocolate–Orange
Sauce (p. 117), **chilled**

Cool the crust completely. Spread the ice cream in an even layer over the crust. Freeze for at least 3 hours. Drizzle the sauce over each slice just before serving.

Pie and torte crusts made from prepared cookies are simple to assemble and don't require baking. Always check the ingredients of the cookies to be sure they don't contain dairy products.

crusts

Okay, so you do need to bake this one, but it's worth the effort when you want an extra-chocolaty, rich dessert. You can also crumble up the baked crust and mix the brownie crumbs into your favorite ice cream.

fudge brownie CRUST

MAKES 1 (9-INCH) SQUARE OR ROUND CRUST

½ cup nonhydrogenated margarine

3 ounces unsweetened chocolate

¾ cup granulated sugar

1 teaspoon vanilla extract

¼ cup plain or vanilla nondairy yogurt

¾ cup whole wheat pastry or unbleached white flour

Preheat the oven to 350 degrees F. Oil a 9-inch square baking dish or 9-inch round cake pan. Combine the margarine and chocolate in a small saucepan and warm on low heat until the chocolate is melted.

Remove from the heat and stir in the sugar and vanilla extract. Then stir in the yogurt. Add the flour and stir until it is just combined; don't overmix. Pour into the prepared pan and bake for 25 minutes. Cool completely before filling.

Vanilla wafers, gingersnaps, and lemon cookies make perfect crusts for fruit-flavored ice creams and sorbets.

cookie CRUST

MAKES 1 (9-INCH) PIE OR TORTE CRUST

1⅔ cups finely crushed cookies of your choice

6 tablespoons vegetable oil or nonhydrogenated margarine, melted

Combine the cookies and oil in a small bowl or food processor and mix until well blended. Press evenly into an unoiled 9-inch pie pan or spring-form pan. Freeze for 15 minutes before filling.

This is a great all-purpose crust. It goes with any flavor.

graham cracker CRUST

MAKES 1 (9-INCH) PIE OR TORTE CRUST

10 whole graham crackers, finely crushed
(about 1½ cups)

3 tablespoons agave syrup or maple syrup

3 tablespoons vegetable oil

Combine the cookies, agave syrup, and oil in a small bowl or food processor and mix until well blended. Press evenly into an unoiled 9-inch pie pan or springform pan. Freeze for 15 minutes before filling.

Dairy-free crème-filled sandwich cookies come in a variety of flavors, such as vanilla cookies with vanilla crème; chocolate cookies with vanilla, peanut butter, or mint crème; and ginger sandwich cookies with vanilla crème. If you're using a food processor to make the crust, you can crush the cookies in the processor before adding the oil.

sandwich cookie CRUST

MAKES 1 (9-INCH) PIE OR TORTE CRUST

18 crème-filled sandwich cookies, finely crushed (1½ cups)

3 tablespoons vegetable oil or nonhydrogenated margarine, melted

Combine the cookies and oil in a small bowl or food processor and mix until well blended. Press evenly into an unoiled 9-inch pie pan or spring-form pan. Freeze for 15 minutes before filling.

breaking
the mold

BOMBES AND TERRINES

5

Molded desserts are quick and easy to prepare because there's no crust to make. You just pack the ice cream into the mold and freeze it until it is solid. You don't even need special molds to make these desserts—you probably have plenty of containers that will work just fine. I prefer metal because it's easy to unmold with a quick dunk in hot water. Stainless steel mixing bowls work great for bombes, and loaf pans work well for terrines. Small metal prep bowls are ideal for individual servings.

Although the recipe instructions call for metal bowls and molds, glass bowls and pans can also be used. Do not dunk them in hot water, however, or they might crack. Place a glass dish in a few inches of cold water for a minute or two, or leave it at room temperature until the dessert slips out when the dish is inverted. Plastic containers also work, but they tend to crack after being frozen a few times. Most books I've read recommend lining the mold with plastic wrap or parchment paper, but I've found that the desserts unmold fine without it.

NOTE: Ice cream and sorbet should be tempered to a spreadable consistency before making a bombe or terrine. However, you do not need to temper ice cream or sorbet that is freshly made and still soft.

molded desserts

This is a very special dessert, perfect for Valentine's Day. If you want even more raspberry flavor, use Chocolate-Raspberry Ice Cream (p. 19) in place of the Chocolate Mousse.

raspberry-chocolate mousse BOMBE

MAKES 12 SERVINGS

1 quart Red Raspberry Sherbet (p. 48)

1 quart Chocolate Mousse Ice Cream (p. 18)

Put a 2-quart metal bowl or mold in the freezer for 15 minutes. Scoop the sherbet into the chilled bowl. Use a soft spatula or wooden spoon to press the sherbet evenly over the bottom and up the sides of the mold, leaving the middle hollow. Freeze for about 30 minutes, or until firm.

Scoop the ice cream into the center of the bowl and press firmly until it is level with the top of the bowl. Cover and freeze for at least 2 hours. To unmold the bombe, dip the pan briefly into hot water and invert it onto a serving plate.

This is perfect for a child's birthday party. For adults, try the variation that follows.

orange cream BOMBE

MAKES 12 SERVINGS

1 quart Orange Sherbet
(p. 49)

1 quart Vanilla Ice Cream
(p. 10)

Put a 2-quart metal bowl or mold in the freezer for 15 minutes. Scoop the sherbet into the chilled bowl. Use a soft spatula or wooden spoon to press the sherbet evenly over the bottom and up the sides of the mold, leaving the middle hollow. Freeze for about 30 minutes, or until firm.

Scoop the ice cream into the center of the bowl and press firmly until it is level with the top of the bowl. Cover and freeze for at least 2 hours. To unmold the bombe, dip the pan briefly into hot water and invert it onto a serving plate.

orange-rosemary bombe: Use Orange Sorbet (p. 61), preferably with the liqueur, instead of the Orange Sherbet, and use Rosemary Ice Cream (p. 31) instead of the Vanilla Ice Cream. Garnish each serving with a sprig of rosemary, if desired.

This is a delicious layered ice-cream cake that both kids and adults love. To make it even more elegant, serve it with Dark Cherry Compote (p. 123).

brownie BOMBE

MAKES 8 SERVINGS

1 quart Vanilla Ice Cream
(p. 10)

2½ cups brownie crumbs

Put a 6-cup metal bowl or mold in the freezer for 15 minutes. Spread 1 cup of the ice cream in an even layer over the bottom of the mold. Top with ¾ cup of the brownie crumbs and pat them down firmly to form an even layer. Spread half of the remaining ice cream evenly over the brownie crumbs. Cover the ice cream with half of the remaining brownie crumbs and pat them down firmly. Spread the remaining ice cream evenly over the brownie crumbs. Top the ice cream with the remaining brownie crumbs and pat them down firmly.

Cover and freeze for at least 3 hours. To unmold the bombe, dip the pan briefly into hot water and invert it onto a serving plate.

This is a delicious, light bombe—perfect for a tea party or luncheon.

fruit and granola BOMBE

MAKES 8 SERVINGS

4½ cups Peach Ice Cream
(p. 43)

2½ cups granola

Put a metal 6-cup bowl or mold in the freezer for 15 minutes. Spread 1½ cups of the ice cream in an even layer over the bottom of the mold. Top with one-third of the granola and pat it down firmly to form an even layer. Spread half of the remaining ice cream evenly over the granola. Cover the ice cream with half of the remaining granola and pat it down firmly. Spread the remaining ice cream evenly over the granola. Top with the remaining granola and pat it down firmly.

Cover and freeze for at least 3 hours. To unmold the bombe, dip the pan briefly into hot water and invert it onto a serving plate.

red, white, and blue granola bombe: Use 1½ cups Blueberry Ice Cream (p. 40) for the first layer, 1½ cups Coconut Ice Cream (p. 27) for the second layer, and 1½ cups Strawberry Ice Cream (p. 38) for the third layer.

I love the flavors of cranberry and orange together. This mix of tartness and creaminess is divine.

cranberry-orange TERRINE

MAKES 10 SERVINGS

3 cups Cranberry-Orange Sorbet (p. 69)

3 cups Orange Ice Cream (p. 45)

Put a metal loaf pan in the freezer for 15 minutes. Press and spread the sorbet into the pan to fill it halfway. If the sorbet is soft, cover and freeze it for 30 minutes, or until it is firm. Press and spread the ice cream over the sorbet to fill the loaf pan completely.

Cover and freeze for at least 3 hours. To unmold the terrine, dip the bowl briefly into hot water and invert it onto a serving plate.

Each slice of this terrine contains all three of the most popular ice-cream flavors. I especially like it drizzled with Fresh Strawberry Sauce (p. 119).

neapolitan ice cream TERRINE

MAKES 10 SERVINGS

2 cups Vanilla Ice Cream (p. 10)

2 cups Chocolate Ice Cream (p. 16)

2 cups Strawberry Ice Cream (p. 38)

Put a metal loaf pan in the freezer for 15 minutes. Press and spread the Vanilla Ice Cream into the bottom of the pan in an even layer. Press and spread the Chocolate Ice Cream evenly over the vanilla layer. Press and spread the Strawberry Ice Cream on top to fill the loaf pan completely.

Cover and freeze for at least 3 hours. To unmold the terrine, dip the pan briefly into hot water and invert it onto a serving plate.

NOTE: If the ice creams are very soft, let each layer harden in the freezer before adding the next layer.

This terrine has a wonderful tropical flavor. The slight spiciness of the lemongrass is cooled by the sweetness of the mango. Use ice cream that is either freshly made or softened slightly so you can spread it. I usually make the sorbet first and spread it in the pan. Then I prepare the ice cream while the first layer is hardening in the freezer.

mango-lemongrass terrine WITH LIME SYRUP

MAKES 10 SERVINGS

MANGO-LEMONGRASS
TERRINE

3 cups Mango Sorbet (p. 68)

3 cups Lemongrass Ice
Cream (p. 32)

LIME SYRUP

5 tablespoons
powdered sugar

5 tablespoons water

Juice and finely
grated peel of 1 lime

To make the terrine, put a metal loaf pan in the freezer for 15 minutes. Press and spread the sorbet into the loaf pan to fill it halfway. If the sorbet is soft, cover and freeze it for 30 minutes, or until it is firm. Press and spread the ice cream over the sorbet to fill the loaf pan completely. Cover and freeze for at least 3 hours.

While the terrine is freezing, and at least 30 minutes before serving time, make the syrup. Whisk together the sugar and water in a small saucepan. Bring to a boil on medium-low heat and boil for 5 minutes, stirring only if necessary to keep the mixture from burning. Stir in the lime juice and peel. Boil for 5 minutes longer, stirring if necessary. Remove from the heat and cool to room temperature.

To unmold the terrine, dip the pan briefly into hot water and invert it onto a serving plate. Drizzle the syrup over the top of the terrine before slicing.

mini bombes

Make lovely, little, individual-serving bombes out of any of the terrine recipes by layering the ice creams in ¾- to 1-cup bowls, cups, or molds.

If you are using freshly made Cherry Sorbet, it may too soft to add the second layer right away. Allow time for it to harden in the mold before adding the Ginger Ice Cream.

cherry-ginger terrine WITH LEMON SAUCE

MAKES 10 SERVINGS

3 cups Cherry Sorbet (p. 65)

3 cups Ginger Ice Cream (p. 28)

1 cup Lemon Sauce (p. 121)

Put a metal loaf pan in the freezer for 15 minutes. Press and spread the sorbet into the pan to fill it halfway. If the sorbet is soft, cover and freeze it for 30 minutes, or until it is firm. Press and spread the ice cream over the sorbet to fill the loaf pan completely. Cover and freeze for at least 3 hours.

While the terrine is freezing, and at least 30 minutes before serving time, prepare the sauce as directed. Cool to room temperature.

To unmold the terrine, dip the bowl briefly into hot water and invert it onto a serving plate. Serve with the sauce.

This is as colorful as it is delicious. To make this terrine even more festive, serve it with Fresh Raspberry Sauce (p. 121).

rainbow sherbet TERRINE

MAKES 10 SERVINGS

2 cups Orange Sherbet (p. 49)

2 cups Lemon-Lime Sherbet (p. 48)

2 cups Red Raspberry Sherbet (p. 48)

Put a metal loaf pan in the freezer for 15 minutes. Press and spread the Orange Sherbet into the bottom of the pan in an even layer. Press and spread the Lemon-Lime Sherbet evenly over the orange layer. Press and spread the Red Raspberry Sherbet on top to fill the loaf pan completely.

Cover and freeze for at least 3 hours. To unmold the terrine, dip the pan briefly into hot water and invert it onto a serving plate.

NOTE: If the sherbets are very soft, let each layer harden in the freezer before adding the next layer.

sweets and treats

6

Looking for an ice-cream snack? This section contains lots of scrumptious sundaes and make-ahead treats like ice pops, drumstick cones, ice-cream sandwiches, and more. Revisit your childhood favorites and indulge in some new treats.

Though I hope you have fun creating your own concoctions using the recipes for ice creams, sauces, and toppings found in this book, I've listed some classic combinations in table 4.

basic ice-cream SUNDAE

Sundaes are delicious any day of the week. Simply place two or three scoops of ice cream (tempered until it can be easily scooped) in a sundae glass, wine goblet, or dessert bowl; drizzle with sauce; and top with the whipped topping of your choice. Garnish with chopped nuts and a cherry, if desired.

TABLE 4 Classic ice-cream sundaes

TYPE OF SUNDAE	ICE CREAM	SAUCE	EXTRAS
Apple Pie Sundae	Cinnamon Ice Cream (p. 30)	Chunky Apple Sauce (p. 119), warm	Maple Walnuts (p. 124)
Blueberry-Peach Crisp Sundae	Rosemary Ice Cream (p. 31)	Chunky Blueberry-Peach Sauce (p. 120), warm	granola
Butterscotch-Peach Sundae	Vanilla Ice Cream (p. 10) or Peach Ice Cream (p. 43)	Butterscotch Sauce (p. 118)	sliced peaches and Maple Walnuts (p. 124)
Hot Fudge Sundae	Vanilla Ice Cream (p. 10) or Mint Ice Cream (p. 15)	Hot Fudge Sauce (p. 116)	chopped walnuts
Mexican Chocolate Sundae	Mexican Chocolate Ice Cream (p. 17)	Chocolate Sauce (p. 117)	Spicy Pecans (p. 125)
Mocha-Almond Sundae	Mocha-Almond Ice Cream (p. 22)	Almond Hot Fudge Sauce (p. 116)	chopped almonds
Peach Melba Sundae	Vanilla Ice Cream (p. 10)	Fresh Raspberry Sauce (p. 121)	sliced peaches
Peanut Butter, Banana, and Chocolate Sundae	Peanut Butter Ice Cream (p. 23)	Chocolate Sauce (p. 117)	sliced bananas and chopped peanuts
Raspberry-Rhubarb Crisp Sundae	Ginger Ice Cream (p. 28)	Raspberry-Rhubarb Sauce (p. 122), warm	granola
Tropical Fruit Sundae	Pineapple Sherbet (p. 50)	Fresh Mango Sauce (p. 122) and Coconut Cream Sauce (p. 123)	sliced bananas and chopped macadamia nuts

Here are a few special sundaes that I've enjoyed at ice-cream parlors in the past. They're simple to make and oh so good.

specialty sundaes

hot fudge brownie sundae

For a luscious treat, place 1 warm or room-temperature brownie in a dessert bowl. Add 2 scoops of your favorite ice cream and top with Hot Fudge Sauce (p. 116) and Whipped Tofu Cream (p. 125).

hot fudge waffle sundae

Sandwich 2 to 3 scoops of Vanilla Ice Cream (p. 10) between two toasted vegan waffles. Top with Hot Fudge Sauce (p. 116).

red, white, and blue parfait sundae

In a tall glass or wine goblet, scoop Vanilla Ice Cream (p. 10) between layers of fresh blueberries and sliced strawberries. Top with granola and Whipped Tofu Cream (p. 125).

classic banana split

Place 1 scoop of Vanilla Ice Cream (p. 10), 1 scoop of Chocolate Ice Cream (p. 16), and 1 scoop of Strawberry Ice Cream (p. 38) side by side in a banana-split dish or dessert bowl. Slice a banana in half lengthwise, and place a half on each side of the ice creams. Spoon Chocolate Sauce (p. 117) on the Vanilla Ice Cream, Strawberry Sauce (p. 119) on the Chocolate Ice Cream, and crushed pineapple on the Strawberry Ice Cream. Top with the whipped topping of your choice, sprinkle with chopped nuts, and garnish with a cherry.

My daughters love to have sundae bars at their parties. I usually offer two or three different ice cream flavors and set out a variety of toppings. I scoop out the ice cream, and the kids add their own toppings.

make-your-own SUNDAE BARS

Here are some of the toppings we like to put out:

- chopped fresh fruit (such as apricots, bananas, mangoes, or peaches)
- chopped, sliced, or slivered nuts (such as almonds, peanuts, or walnuts)
- crumbled cookies or brownies
- dairy-free chocolate, peanut butter, butterscotch, and/or white chocolate chips
- fresh or thawed frozen berries
- granola
- Hot Fudge Sauce (p. 116), Chocolate Sauce (p. 117), and/or any of the other sauces in this book
- shredded dried coconut
- sprinkles
- trail mix
- vegan marshmallows
- Whipped Cashew Cream (p. 124) or Whipped Tofu Cream (p. 125)

Kids love these little sundae cups. I keep a few in my freezer for when my daughters have friends over. One-cup glass prep bowls with fitted lids can be found at most kitchen supply stores, and small plastic containers can usually be found wherever there's a good selection of plasticware—just make sure they're freezerproof or they'll crack after one or two uses.

ice-cream SUNDAE CUPS

MAKES 6 SUNDAE CUPS

1 quart Vanilla Ice Cream
(p. 10), **slightly softened**

1/3 cup dark or semisweet
chocolate chips

1 tablespoon vegetable oil

3 tablespoons chopped nuts
(such as almonds, peanuts,
pecans, or walnuts)

Have ready six ³/4- to 1-cup containers and scoop about ²/3 cup of ice cream into each one. If the ice cream is freshly made and soft, freeze the filled containers for 1 hour, or until the ice cream is firm.

Melt the chocolate chips and oil together in a double boiler over gently simmering water or in a glass bowl in the microwave. Stir until smooth. Working with 1 container at a time, spoon 1 tablespoon of the melted chocolate over the ice cream. Immediately sprinkle with 1¹/2 teaspoons of the chopped nuts. Cover the sundae cups and store in the freezer until ready to serve. Temper at room temperature for about 10 minutes before serving.

Although I've included my favorite ice-pop recipes in this section, all of the sorbet bases in this book make excellent ice pops as well. Just mix them up, pour them into pop molds, and freeze. I also like to use leftover ice cream or frozen yogurt to make ice pops. That way, when my kids want a snack, they don't have to wait for the ice cream to temper. It's a little tricky to get ice cream into the molds without air pockets. Use a small spoon to fill the mold with the ice cream, then poke the ice cream with a butter knife a few times to remove any air bubbles.

making perfect ice pops

One day when I was testing both the Spiced Apple Sorbet and the Vanilla Frozen Yogurt, I used the leftovers to create these pops. My family loved them so much that I had to include the recipe here for you to try also. Apple juice will work in place of the sorbet in a pinch, but you'll need to freeze that layer before you add the frozen yogurt.

apple pie à la mode POPS

MAKES 8 (2-OUNCE) POPS

1 cup softened Spiced Apple Sorbet (p. 70)

1 cup softened Vanilla Frozen Yogurt (p. 57) or Vanilla Ice Cream (p. 10)

Fill the pop molds halfway with the sorbet. Fill the remainder with the frozen yogurt or ice cream. Poke the pops with a butter knife a few times to remove any air bubbles. It's okay if the flavors swirl together a little. Freeze for at least 4 hours or the sticks may pull out when the pops are removed from the molds.

These make wonderfully healthful and delicious treats. I keep them in my freezer all summer long for the kids to snack on.

pomegranate-strawberry POPS

MAKES 8 (2-OUNCE) POPS

1 cup pomegranate juice

¾ cup diced strawberries

2 tablespoons agave syrup

Combine all of the ingredients in a blender and process until smooth. Pour into pop molds and freeze.

When watermelon is blended, it turns into juice. The yogurt adds creaminess and a pleasant tang. The freshly blended mixture is also delicious as a smoothie.

watermelon yogurt POPS

MAKES 8 (2-OUNCE) POPS

2 ½ cups diced seedless watermelon

½ cup plain or vanilla nondairy yogurt

Combine the watermelon and yogurt in a blender and process until smooth. Pour into pop molds and freeze.

watermelon-raspberry yogurt pops: Replace ½ cup of the diced watermelon with ½ cup of raspberries.

If you like lemonade, you'll love these refreshing pops.

lemonade POPS

MAKES 8 (2-OUNCE) POPS

6 tablespoons freshly
squeezed lemon juice

1/4 cup agave syrup

1/4 cup boiling water

1 cup cold water

Combine the lemon juice, agave syrup, and boiling water in a heatproof bowl or large measuring cup. Stir in the cold water. Pour into pop molds and freeze.

These delicious pops have no sweeteners added—they're all fruit.

blueberry-banana-apple POPS

MAKES 8 (2-OUNCE) POPS

1 banana

1/2 cup blueberries

1/2 cup apple juice

Combine all of the ingredients in a blender and process until smooth. Pour into pop molds and freeze.

blueberry-banana yogurt pops: Replace the apple juice with 1/2 cup of vanilla nondairy yogurt.

We also call these mango lassi pops, after the popular Indian drink, because that's exactly what they taste like.

mango yogurt POPS

MAKES 8 (2-OUNCE) POPS

1 cup vanilla or peach nondairy yogurt

1½ cups mango chunks

Combine all of the ingredients in a blender and process until smooth. Pour into pop molds and freeze.

orange-mango pops: Use 1 cup freshly squeezed orange juice in place of the yogurt.

When you want something other than fruit pops, these will do the trick. They are especially good with a chocolate coating (see p. 99).

vanilla yogurt POPS

MAKES 8 (2-OUNCE) POPS

1½ cups vanilla nondairy yogurt

½ cup soymilk or other nondairy milk

1 tablespoon agave syrup

Combine all of the ingredients in a blender and process until smooth. Pour into pop molds and freeze.

vanana yogurt pops: Add 1 banana, peeled and broken into chunks, in place of the agave syrup.

This is a delicious way to use up any leftover Whipped Tofu Cream. These pops taste like a strawberry milk shake.

strawberry cream POPS

⅔ cup Whipped Tofu Cream (p. 125)

1¼ cups halved strawberries

½ cup apple juice

Combine all of the ingredients in a blender and process until smooth. Pour into pop molds and freeze.

These dark chocolate fudge pops taste just like the ones I got from the ice-cream truck when I was a kid.

fudge POPS

1¾ cups soymilk or other nondairy milk

⅓ cup granulated sugar

3 tablespoons unsweetened cocoa powder

⅓ cup semisweet chocolate chips

½ teaspoon vanilla extract

Pour the soymilk into a small saucepan. Whisk in the sugar and cocoa powder. Warm on medium heat until the soymilk begins to simmer. Remove from the heat and stir in the chocolate chips and vanilla extract. Cool to room temperature. Pour into pop molds and freeze.

Turn any ice pop into a chocolate-covered treat. We especially like this with Vanilla Yogurt Pops (p. 97), Vanana Yogurt Pops (p. 97), and Strawberry Cream Pops (p. 98). And for you chocoholics, try this with Fudge Pops (p. 98).

chocolate-covered POPS

MAKES 8 TO 10 (2-OUNCE) POPS

8 to 10 (2-ounce)
ice pops, frozen solid

1¾ cups Hardening
Chocolate Sauce (p. 118)

Line a large baking sheet with parchment paper and put it in the freezer 10 minutes before you plan to start. Unmold the ice pops and place them on a plate in the freezer. Remove the parchment-lined baking sheet. Working quickly, with 1 pop at a time, dip each pop in the chocolate sauce until it is coated. Let the excess sauce drip off and place the coated pop on the parchment-lined sheet. As the chocolate sauce dwindles, you will need to spoon it over the remaining ice pops. Eat the pops immediately or store them in the freezer.

variation: Place 1 cup of chopped nuts on a plate. After you dip each pop in the chocolate sauce, immediately roll it in the nuts.

This was my favorite treat from the ice-cream truck when I was a kid. This homemade version is as much fun to make as it is to eat.

drumstick CONES

MAKES 8 CONES

1 quart ice cream, slightly softened but still firm

8 sugar cones

1¾ cups Hardening Chocolate Sauce (p. 118)

1 cup chopped nuts (such as almonds, peanuts, pecans, or walnuts)

Line a large baking sheet with parchment paper and put it in the freezer 10 minutes before you plan to start. Spoon some ice cream into a cone, then place a rounded scoop on top of the cone and pack the ice cream down firmly (a ¼-cup ice-cream scoop works well for this). Carefully place the cone on the baking sheet in the freezer. Repeat with the remaining cones. Freeze for at least 2 hours. They must be frozen very hard before they are dipped or the ice cream will fall out of the cones.

Place the nuts in small bowl. Working with 1 cone at a time, take the cone out of the freezer. Tilt the bowl or saucepan of Hardening Chocolate Sauce to create a deep pool and quickly dip the ice-cream end of the cone into the chocolate. Shake gently to let the excess drip back into the bowl. Immediately press the chocolate-covered ice cream into the nuts. Return the cone to the baking sheet in the freezer. Freeze for at least 10 minutes before serving. The cones can be eaten immediately or stored in heavy-duty zipper-lock plastic bags in the freezer.

Although this recipe calls for Vanilla Ice Cream, almost any flavor would be delicious. Our favorites are Mint Ice Cream (p. 15), Coffee Ice Cream (p. 21), and Chocolate-Raspberry Ice Cream (p. 19).

chocolate-covered BONBONS

2 cups Vanilla Ice Cream (p. 10)

¾ cup dark or semisweet chocolate chips

2 tablespoons vegetable oil

Line a baking sheet with parchment paper and put it in the freezer 10 minutes before you plan to start. Use a melon baller to scoop balls of ice cream and place them on the baking sheet. Return the baking sheet to the freezer and freeze for 1 hour, or until very firm.

Melt the chocolate chips and oil together in a double boiler over gently simmering water or in a glass bowl in the microwave. Stir until smooth. Spoon the melted chocolate over each ball so most of the ice cream is coated. Serve immediately or store in the freezer.

nutty chocolate-covered bonbons: Sprinkle each ice-cream ball with chopped nuts of your choice immediately after spooning on the melted chocolate.

This is a fun dessert for kids but elegant enough for adults. Snowballs look very attractive served in a glass bowl or martini glass.

snowballs

MAKES 6 SNOWBALLS

1 quart Vanilla Ice Cream (p. 10)

2 cups unsweetened shredded dried coconut

If the ice cream is freshly made, harden it in the freezer until it is firm enough to scoop. If the ice cream is frozen solid, temper it in the refrigerator for 30 minutes, or until it is soft enough to scoop.

Line a baking sheet with parchment paper and put it in the freezer 10 minutes before you plan to start. Place the coconut in a small bowl. Scoop a ball of ice cream (about ⅔ cup) and drop it into the coconut. Use a spoon to roll it around until it is completely coated with coconut. Place it on the chilled baking sheet. Repeat with the remaining ice cream and coconut. Serve immediately or store in the freezer.

These decadent bars taste like brownie sundaes.

white chocolate brownie BARS

MAKES 16 BARS

1 Fudge Brownie Crust (p. 78), prepared in a 9-inch square baking pan

1 quart White Chocolate Ice Cream (p. 20), slightly softened

¾ cup mini dark or semisweet chocolate chips

Bake the crust according to the recipe directions and cool completely. Spread the ice cream over the cooled crust to fill the baking pan. Sprinkle the chocolate chips evenly over the ice cream and press them in slightly. Freeze for at least 3 hours before serving.

Use any flavor of ice cream you like in these bars—our favorites (so far) are Coconut Ice Cream (p. 27), Low-Fat Strawberry-Banana Ice Cream (p. 53), and Cinnamon Ice Cream (p. 30).

ice-cream granola BARS

MAKES 16 BARS

2 cups granola

¾ cup Chocolate Sauce (p. 117) or chocolate syrup

1 to 1¼ quarts freshly made ice cream

Spread 1 cup of the granola in the bottom of a 9-inch square baking dish. Drizzle half of the chocolate sauce over the granola. Scoop the ice cream over the granola and sauce and carefully press it into the pan to form an even layer. Drizzle the remaining chocolate sauce over the ice cream. Sprinkle the remaining cup of granola over the top and press it in slightly. Freeze for at least 3 hours before serving.

Tart lemon ice cream on a shortbread crust—just like grandma used to make, except colder. If you want these to be even more lemony, serve them with Lemon Sauce (p. 121).

lemon BARS

MAKES 16 BARS

1 cup whole wheat pastry or unbleached white flour

¼ cup powdered sugar

½ cup nonhydrogenated margarine

1 quart Lemon Ice Cream (p. 46), slightly softened

Preheat the oven to 350 degrees F. Lightly oil a 9-inch square baking pan. Stir together the flour and sugar or pulse them together in a food processor. Using a pastry blender, your hands, or a food processor, work in the margarine until the dough resembles coarse meal. Squeeze some in your hands to make sure it holds together. If it doesn't, add a little ice water. Press the dough evenly into the bottom of the prepared pan. Bake for 20 minutes, or until golden around the edges. Cool completely.

Scoop the ice cream into the cooled crust and carefully press it into the pan to form an even layer. Freeze for at least 3 hours before serving.

Ice-cream sandwiches are easy to make, and kids love them. Chocolate chip cookies are probably the most common ice-cream sandwich cookie, but also try oatmeal cookies, molasses cookies, snickerdoodles, or any kind of cookie you like.

ice-cream sandwiches

To make an ice-cream sandwich, simply scoop your favorite flavor of ice cream onto one cookie and press another cookie on top. The ice cream should be fairly firm, so you may need to harden it a bit so it won't ooze right out.

To make ice-cream sandwiches even more special, roll the edges in mini chocolate chips or chopped nuts. After making the sandwiches, place them in the freezer to harden for at least 2 hours before serving. If you will be storing them for just a short time, put several in a large freezer container. If you will be storing them for a few days or longer, wrap each one individually in a heavy-duty zipper-lock plastic bag to prevent freezer burn.

This is a fun way to dress up your ice-cream sandwiches.

chocolate-dipped ICE-CREAM SANDWICHES

MAKES 10 SANDWICHES

1¾ cups Hardening Chocolate Sauce (p. 118)

10 ice-cream sandwiches (see p. 104), **frozen solid**

Line a baking sheet with parchment paper and put it in the freezer 10 minutes before you plan to start. Working with 1 sandwich at a time, dip it in the chocolate sauce so that half the sandwich is coated. Let the excess sauce drip off, then place the sandwich on the parchment-lined sheet. Let the chocolate-coated sandwiches rest for 5 minutes, or until the chocolate is hard. Serve immediately or store in the freezer.

bottoms up

SHAKES, SODAS, AND FLOATS

7

Ice cream can be as much fun to drink as it is to eat. Buy a big box of straws and get ready to start slurping. Here are recipes for sweet, thick slushies; creamy shakes; fizzy sodas; and both cold and hot floats.

This is a delicious, wholesome alternative to those sugary drinks with artificial coloring sold at carnivals and convenience stores.

watermelon SLUSHY

8 cups diced watermelon

¼ cup agave syrup

Place the diced watermelon in a food processor or blender and process until smooth. Place a fine-mesh strainer over a medium bowl and pour the blended watermelon through it to remove the seeds (you should have about 4 cups of watermelon juice). Whisk in the agave syrup. If the watermelon was cold, the mixture may be frozen immediately; otherwise, chill it in the refrigerator for at least 2 hours. Freeze in an ice-cream maker until thick and slushy, about 20 minutes.

This is a great treat for adults. For a fun presentation, serve it in salt-rimmed margarita glasses.

margarita SLUSHY

1½ cups granulated sugar

2 cups boiling water

Juice of 3 medium lemons
(a little less than ¾ cup)

Juice of 4 medium limes
(about ½ cup)

2 tablespoons tequila

2 tablespoons Triple Sec

Place the sugar in a heatproof bowl. Pour the boiling water over the sugar and whisk until it is dissolved. Whisk in the lemon and lime juices. Cool slightly. Chill in the refrigerator for 3 hours, or until cold. Whisk in the tequila and Triple Sec. Freeze in an ice-cream maker until thick and slushy, about 20 minutes.

There is nothing quite as soothing and satisfying as a pure vanilla shake.

very vanilla SHAKE

4 scoops (about 1½ cups) **Vanilla Ice Cream** (p. 10)

¾ **cup soymilk or other nondairy milk**

¼ **teaspoon vanilla extract**

Combine all of the ingredients in a blender and process until smooth.

This classic shake is rich and chocolaty. Serve it with a veggie burger and sweet potato fries for a complete diner-meal experience.

chocolate SHAKE

MAKES 1 TO 2 SERVINGS

4 scoops (about 1½ cups) **Chocolate Ice Cream** (p. 16)

¾ cup soymilk or other nondairy milk

4 teaspoons Chocolate Sauce (p. 117) **or chocolate syrup**

Combine all of the ingredients in a blender and process until smooth.

chocolate-almond shake: Add 1 tablespoon of almond butter.

chocolate-hazelnut shake: Add 1 tablespoon Frangelico liqueur.

chocolate-mint shake: Add ¼ teaspoon of peppermint extract.

chocolate–peanut butter shake: Add 1 tablespoon of peanut butter.

Before I got married I worked at a natural food deli. This was our most popular smoothie.

almond dream SHAKE

MAKES 1 TO 2 SERVINGS

2 scoops (about ¾ cup) **Vanilla Frozen Yogurt** (p. 57)

1 large banana, peeled, sliced, and frozen

1 cup soymilk or other nondairy milk

2 tablespoons almond butter

Combine all of the ingredients in a blender and process until smooth.

This is so very good—creamy and bursting with strawberries.

ultimate strawberry SHAKE

MAKES 1 TO 2 SERVINGS

3 scoops (a little more than 1 cup) **Strawberry Ice Cream** (p. 38)

1 cup halved strawberries

½ cup soymilk or other nondairy milk

Combine all of the ingredients in a blender and process until smooth.

blueberry shake: Use Blueberry Ice Cream (p. 40) instead of Strawberry Ice Cream and substitute blueberries for the strawberries.

peach shake: Use Peach Ice Cream (p. 43) instead of Strawberry Ice Cream and substitute peaches for the strawberries.

This is like a thick, rich, iced coffee—just as good as the drinks you get at a coffeehouse.

coffee SHAKE

MAKES 1 TO 2 SERVINGS

4 scoops (about 1½ cups) **Coffee Ice Cream** (p. 21)

¾ **cup soymilk or other nondairy milk**

½ **teaspoon instant coffee granules or powdered coffee substitute**

Combine all of the ingredients in a blender and process until smooth.

Kahlúa coffee shake: Use 1 to 2 tablespoons of Kahlúa liqueur instead of the instant coffee.

mocha shake: Use Chocolate Ice Cream (p. 16) instead of Coffee Ice Cream.

Ice-cream sodas are sweet and bubbly, and really fun to eat.

vanilla ice-cream SODA

4 tablespoons soy creamer

2 tablespoons agave syrup

¼ teaspoon vanilla extract

1 cup cold seltzer water

1 large scoop Vanilla Ice Cream (p. 10)

Place the soy creamer, agave syrup, and vanilla extract into a tall glass. Stir until combined. Add the seltzer water and give the mixture a few stirs; it may froth a bit. Gently press the scoop of ice cream onto the rim of the glass. Serve with a long-handled iced-tea spoon and a straw.

It's hard to find an ice-cream parlor that serves real ice-cream sodas anymore, but I just love them—especially chocolate.

chocolate ice-cream SODA

MAKES 1 SERVING

2 tablespoons soy creamer

2 tablespoons Chocolate Sauce (p. 117) or chocolate syrup

1 cup cold seltzer water

1 large scoop Chocolate Ice Cream (p. 16)

Place the creamer and chocolate sauce into a tall glass. Stir until combined. Add the seltzer water and give the mixture a few stirs; it may froth a bit. Gently press the scoop of ice cream onto the rim of the glass. Serve with a long-handled iced-tea spoon and a straw.

My kids really love this ice-cream soda. It's a fun snack they can make themselves.

strawberry ice-cream SODA

MAKES 1 SERVING

2 tablespoons soy creamer

2 tablespoons Fresh Strawberry Sauce (p. 121)

1 cup cold seltzer water

1 large scoop Strawberry Ice Cream (p. 38)

Place the creamer and strawberry sauce into a tall glass. Stir until combined. Add the seltzer water and give the mixture a few stirs; it may froth a bit. Gently press the scoop of ice cream onto the rim of the glass. Serve with a long-handled iced-tea spoon and a straw.

This is like a bubbly iced coffee—sweet, with a little kick.

coffee ice-cream SODA

MAKES 1 SERVING

3 tablespoons soy creamer

1½ tablespoons agave syrup

½ teaspoon instant coffee granules or powdered coffee substitute

1 cup cold seltzer water

1 large scoop Coffee Ice Cream (p. 21)

Place the creamer, agave syrup, and instant coffee granules into a tall glass. Add the seltzer water and give the mixture a few stirs; it may froth a bit. Gently press the scoop of ice cream onto the rim of the glass. Serve with a long-handled iced-tea spoon and a straw.

mocha ice-cream soda: Substitute Chocolate Ice Cream (p. 16) for the Coffee Ice Cream.

I wasn't able to find an all-natural orange soda for this float, so I came up with my own. Not only is it nutritious, it tastes great in this float.

orange cream FLOAT

MAKES 1 SERVING

⅔ cup sparkling water or seltzer water

⅓ cup freshly squeezed orange juice

Agave syrup (optional)

1 large scoop Vanilla Ice Cream (p. 10)

Combine the sparkling water and orange juice in a tall glass. Add a little agave syrup to sweeten, if desired. Gently drop the scoop of ice cream into the soda. Serve with a long-handled iced-tea spoon and a straw.

Who needs marshmallows! Try a scoop of ice cream in your hot chocolate instead.

hot chocolate FLOAT

MAKES 4 SERVINGS

3 cups soymilk or other nondairy milk

1 cup dark or semisweet chocolate chips

¼ teaspoon vanilla extract

4 scoops Vanilla Ice Cream (p. 10)

Place the soymilk and chocolate chips in a saucepan on medium-low heat. Heat, whisking occasionally, until the soymilk just starts to boil. Remove from the heat, add the vanilla extract, and whisk until smooth and foamy. Pour evenly into 4 mugs. Carefully drop a scoop of the ice cream into each mug.

In case you thought ice cream was only for summer, here's a way to stay warm and still enjoy your ice cream.

hot apple cider FLOAT

MAKES 8 TO 12 SERVINGS

½ gallon apple cider

1 teaspoon whole allspice

1 teaspoon whole cloves

1 (3-inch) cinnamon stick

1 quart Vanilla Ice Cream (p. 10) or Cinnamon Ice Cream (p. 30)

Cinnamon sticks for garnish (optional)

Pour the cider into a medium saucepan. Stir in the allspice, cloves, and cinnamon stick. Cover and bring to a boil on medium-high heat. Reduce the heat to low and simmer, covered, for 20 minutes.

Place a fine-mesh strainer over a large bowl and pour the mixture through it to remove the spices. Pour the hot cider into large mugs, filling them about three-quarters full. Carefully place a scoop of the ice cream in each mug. Garnish with additional cinnamon sticks, if desired.

all the extras

SAUCES, TOPPINGS, AND MIX-INS

8

This section includes lots of sauces and toppings for your sundaes and ice-cream desserts. You'll find dairy-free versions of classics, like hot fudge sauce and butterscotch sauce, and a variety of sauces made with fresh fruit. There are also whipped toppings, sweetened and spiced nuts, and even truffles to mix into your ice cream. Many of these are included in other recipes throughout the book, but you can also have fun using them to create your own unique desserts.

This luscious sauce is thick and gooey and chocolaty. It's the perfect topping for almost any ice cream.

hot fudge SAUCE

MAKES 1 CUP

¼ cup nonhydrogenated margarine

2 ounces unsweetened chocolate

6 tablespoons cocoa powder

¾ cup granulated sugar

½ cup soy creamer

Combine the margarine and chocolate in a small saucepan on low heat. Heat, whisking occasionally, until the margarine and chocolate are melted. Remove from the heat and whisk in the cocoa powder. Then whisk in the sugar. Finally, whisk in the soy creamer. Warm on low heat until the sugar is dissolved and the sauce is hot. Serve warm.

almond hot fudge sauce: Add ¼ teaspoon almond extract along with the soy creamer.

mint hot fudge sauce: Add ⅛ teaspoon peppermint extract along with the soy creamer.

orange hot fudge sauce: Add ⅛ teaspoon orange extract along with the soy creamer.

NOTE: This sauce can be cooled and stored in the refrigerator for up to three weeks. I recommend storing it in a heatproof glass jar (like a canning jar). To reheat it, place the uncovered jar in a saucepan of gently simmering water or in the microwave.

This sauce is quick to whip up and keeps for several weeks in the refrigerator. It's an easy way for your kids to dress up their ice cream.

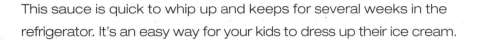

chocolate SAUCE

MAKES ABOUT 1 CUP

½ cup cocoa powder

½ cup maple syrup

1 to 1½ tablespoons soymilk or other nondairy milk

¾ teaspoon vanilla extract

Combine all of the ingredients in a small bowl and mix with a fork until smooth.

We love this rich, creamy sauce over any of the chocolate ice creams.

white chocolate SAUCE

MAKES ABOUT 2 CUPS

1 (14-ounce) can full-fat coconut milk (cream only)

¾ cup white chocolate chips

Open the can of coconut milk and carefully scoop out the hard white cream on top. Discard the liquid. Place the coconut cream in a small saucepan and heat until it just starts to simmer. Remove from the heat and whisk in the chocolate chips until smooth. Chill in the refrigerator for several hours, until the sauce is cold.

white chocolate–orange sauce: Whisk ⅛ teaspoon of orange extract into the sauce before chilling it. If you like, also add 2 tablespoons of Grand Marnier.

This amazing sauce hardens to a crispy shell as it coats the ice cream. Store leftover sauce in a heatproof jar in the refrigerator. Shortly before serving, warm the sauce in the microwave or place the jar in a pan of gently simmering water until the sauce is melted.

hardening chocolate SAUCE

MAKES 1¾ CUPS

1½ cups dark or semisweet chocolate chips (one 10-ounce package)

¼ cup vegetable oil

Melt the chocolate chips and oil together in a double boiler over gently simmering water or in a glass bowl in the microwave. Whisk until smooth. Serve warm.

In order to get the requisite caramelized-sugar taste, don't stir this sauce until the instructions tell you to.

butterscotch SAUCE

MAKES 1 CUP

½ cup turbinado, raw, or brown sugar

6 tablespoons maple syrup

2 tablespoons nonhydrogenated margarine

1 teaspoon vanilla extract

¼ teaspoon salt

⅓ cup soy creamer

Combine the sugar and maple syrup in a small saucepan on medium-low heat. Stir constantly until the sugar dissolves. Raise the heat to medium-high and bring to a boil. Boil for 5 minutes; do not stir. Remove from the heat and add the margarine, vanilla extract, and salt, but still do not stir. Let the mixture rest for 5 minutes. Then beat or whisk in the soy creamer until the sauce is smooth and creamy. Serve warm or cold.

This easy sauce is a real treat in summer with fresh, ripe berries. It's eye-catching and delectable over Vanilla Bean Ice Cream (p. 12) and Lemon Ice Cream (p. 46).

fresh strawberry SAUCE

MAKES ABOUT 1¼ CUPS

2 cups quartered strawberries

1½ tablespoons granulated sugar or agave syrup

1 teaspoon freshly squeezed lemon juice

Combine all of the ingredients in a blender or food processor and process until smooth. For an extra-smooth sauce, place a fine-mesh strainer over a medium bowl and press the mixture through it to remove the seeds. Serve chilled or at room temperature. Store leftover sauce in a covered container in the refrigerator for up to 5 days.

Warm, sweet, and bursting with cinnamon—this is the perfect fall topping for Vanilla Ice Cream (p. 10) or any herb-flavored ice cream.

chunky apple SAUCE

MAKES ABOUT 3 CUPS

5 cups peeled and diced apples

½ cup apple juice or water

1 tablespoon maple syrup or brown sugar

½ teaspoon ground cinnamon

Dash ground nutmeg

Place the apples and juice in a medium saucepan. Drizzle the maple syrup over the apples and sprinkle with the cinnamon and nutmeg. Cook on medium-low heat, stirring occasionally, for 10 to 15 minutes, until the apples soften. Serve warm or cold.

This sauce tastes like peach pie. We like to serve it warm over Vanilla Ice Cream (p. 10) or Rosemary Ice Cream (p. 31).

chunky peach SAUCE

6 medium peaches, diced (see note)

3 tablespoons water

2 tablespoons granulated sugar or agave syrup

⅛ teaspoon ground cardamom

Place the peaches and water in a saucepan. Drizzle the sugar over the peaches and sprinkle with the cardamom. Bring to a boil, stirring occasionally. Reduce the heat to low, cover, and simmer for 10 to 15 minutes, or until the peaches are tender. Serve warm or cold.

chunky blueberry-peach sauce: When the peaches are tender, remove from the heat and gently stir in ½ cup of blueberries. Cover and let rest for 10 minutes.

chunky nectarine sauce: Replace the peaches with 4 cups of diced nectarines.

NOTE: I like the flavor of the peel in this sauce, but if it is very thick or unattractive, pull it off as you dice the fruit.

Try this beautiful red sauce over Vanilla Bean Ice Cream (p. 12), Peach Ice Cream (p. 43), or Chocolate Ice Cream (p. 16).

fresh raspberry SAUCE

MAKES 1 CUP

2 cups raspberries

3 tablespoons agave syrup

Combine the raspberries and agave syrup in a blender and process until smooth. Place a fine-mesh strainer over a medium bowl and press the mixture through it to remove the seeds. Serve chilled or at room temperature. Store leftover sauce in a covered container in the refrigerator for up to 3 days.

This sauce goes well with fruity or herb-flavored ice creams. Use an organic lemon, if possible.

lemon SAUCE

MAKES 1 CUP

1 cup water

6 tablespoons granulated sugar

Juice and grated peel of 1 lemon

2 tablespoons arrowroot powder

Place all of the ingredients in a small saucepan and whisk to combine. Bring to a boil on medium heat, whisking frequently to keep the sauce from burning. Reduce the heat to low and simmer for 5 to 10 minutes, until the sauce has thickened. Serve warm or cold.

lime sauce: Use 2 medium limes and their grated peel instead of the lemon juice and lemon peel.

This tropical sauce tastes great over Pineapple Sherbet (p. 50) or Coconut Ice Cream (p. 27).

fresh mango SAUCE

MAKES 2 CUPS

2 cups mango chunks

2 tablespoons freshly squeezed orange juice

Combine the mango and juice in a blender and process until smooth. Chill in the refrigerator before serving.

This slightly tart sauce has a beautiful pink and red color. Try it over Ginger Ice Cream (p. 28).

raspberry-rhubarb SAUCE

MAKES 2½ CUPS

3 cups sliced rhubarb (½-inch slices)

½ cup granulated sugar or agave syrup

¼ cup water

⅛ teaspoon ground ginger

1 cup raspberries

Combine the rhubarb, sugar, water, and ginger in a saucepan and bring to a boil, stirring occasionally. Reduce the heat to low, cover, and simmer for 10 minutes. Gently stir in the raspberries, cover, and simmer for 2 to 3 minutes longer, or until the rhubarb is tender. Serve warm or cold.

This sauce adds a tropical flavor to frozen desserts. We love it over fruit ice creams and sorbets.

coconut cream SAUCE

MAKES ABOUT 1 CUP

1 (14-ounce) can full-fat coconut milk (cream only)

2 tablespoons agave syrup or powdered sugar

1 teaspoon vanilla extract

Open the can of coconut milk and carefully scoop out the hard white cream on top. Discard the liquid. Place the coconut cream in a bowl. Add the agave syrup and vanilla extract and whisk or beat until the sauce is smooth. Chill in the refrigerator for at least 1 hour before serving.

Use fresh or frozen cherries to make this luscious sauce. Use it to top Vanilla Ice Cream (p. 10) or Chocolate Ice Cream (p. 16).

dark cherry COMPOTE

MAKES 2 CUPS

3 cups pitted dark cherries

¼ cup freshly squeezed orange juice

1 to 2 tablespoons granulated sugar or agave syrup

2 tablespoons Kirsch liqueur (optional)

Combine the cherries, juice, and sugar in a saucepan and bring to a boil, stirring occasionally. Reduce the heat to low, cover, and simmer for 10 minutes, or until the cherries are tender. Remove from the heat and stir in the liqueur, if using. Serve warm or cold.

Cashews are amazingly creamy and make a wonderful, thick topping similar to whipped cream.

WHIPPED **cashew cream**

1½ cups raw cashews

½ cup rice milk

2 tablespoons maple syrup or agave syrup

2 teaspoons vanilla extract

Place the cashews in a blender and grind them into a powder. Add the rice milk, maple syrup, and vanilla extract and process until smooth. Chill in the refrigerator for 1 hour, or until cold and firm.

whipped orange-cashew cream: Add ⅛ teaspoon of orange extract along with the vanilla extract.

These sweet, crispy nuts are wonderful over Vanilla Ice Cream (p. 10), Pumpkin Spice Ice Cream (p. 32), Cinnamon Ice Cream (p. 30), or just about any other ice cream you fancy. For easier cleanup, line the baking sheet with parchment paper.

maple walnuts

2 cups walnuts

3 tablespoons maple syrup

Preheat the oven to 350 degrees F. Spread the walnuts in a single layer on a baking sheet and bake them for 10 minutes. Do not turn off the oven.

While the walnuts are still warm, put them into a colander and rub them against the sides to remove the skins. (Use a clean dish cloth or towel to keep from burning your hands.)

Transfer the walnuts to a medium bowl. Add the maple syrup and stir until the walnuts are evenly coated. Arrange the walnuts in a single layer on the baking sheet and bake for 8 minutes. Remove from the oven and use a spatula to stir the walnuts and spread them into a single layer again. Bake for 2 to 5 minutes longer, or until golden. Cool completely. Store in a covered jar at room temperature.

This is a delicious, nondairy alternative to whipped cream. Keep blending until it is very creamy.

WHIPPED **tofu cream**

MAKES ABOUT 1⅓ CUPS

1 (12-ounce) package
firm silken tofu

3 tablespoons maple syrup
or agave syrup

2 tablespoons vegetable oil

1 teaspoon vanilla extract

Combine all of the ingredients in a blender or food processor and process until very smooth and creamy. Chill in the refrigerator for at least 1 hour, or until cold and firm.

whipped tofu almond cream: Add ¼ teaspoon of almond extract along with the vanilla extract.

whipped tofu chocolate cream: Add 2 tablespoons of unsweetened cocoa powder.

These sweet-and-spicy nuts are a delicious contrast to cold, creamy ice cream. I especially like them with Chocolate Ice Cream (p. 16).

spicy pecans

MAKES 2 CUPS

2 cups pecans

1 tablespoon maple syrup

2 teaspoons salt

½ teaspoon crushed
red pepper flakes

½ teaspoon chili powder

½ teaspoon cayenne

½ teaspoon chili paste

Preheat the oven to 300 degrees F and line a baking sheet with parchment paper. Combine the pecans, maple syrup, 1 teaspoon of the salt, and all of the red pepper flakes, chili powder, cayenne, and chili paste. Stir until the pecans are evenly coated.

Spread the pecans in a single layer on the prepared baking sheet and bake for 20 minutes. Remove from the oven and toss with the remaining teaspoon of salt. Cool completely. Store in a covered jar at room temperature.

These easy truffles are delicious mixed into your favorite ice cream. Make them when you prepare the ice-cream base so they can harden while the base is chilling. Table 1 (p. 8) provides a list of liqueurs and their flavors. Choose a liqueur whose flavor complements the ice cream you will be adding the truffles to.

chocolate TRUFFLES

**MAKES ABOUT ¾ CUP CHOPPED TRUFFLES
(ENOUGH TO MIX INTO 1 QUART OF ICE CREAM)**

¼ cup soy creamer

1 tablespoon nonhydrogenated margarine or coconut oil

4 ounces dark or semi-sweet chocolate, broken or chopped into pieces

1 tablespoon liqueur of your choice

Line a small, shallow pan or bowl with parchment paper. Place the creamer and margarine in a small saucepan and warm on medium heat until the margarine is melted and bubbles form around the edge of the pan.

Remove from the heat and whisk in the chocolate until smooth. Then whisk in the liqueur. Pour into the prepared pan and cool in the refrigerator until firm. Chop or break the truffles into small pieces before adding them to the ice cream of your choice.

suppliers

Cooking.com

www.cooking.com
4086 Del Rey Avenue
Marina Del Rey, CA 90292
800-663-8810

Ice-cream makers and other kitchen appliances, cookware, and bakeware.

Cosmo's Vegan Shoppe

www.cosmosveganshoppe.com
1860 Sandy Plains Road, Suite 204–208
Marietta, GA 30066
800-260-9968

Vegan marshmallows, chocolate chips, white chocolate chips, chocolate syrup, truffles, and candy.

Cuisinart

www.cuisinart.com
150 Milford Road
East Windsor, NJ 08520
800-726-0190

Ice-cream makers, food processors, and blenders.

Cuisipro

www.cuisipro.com
802 Centerpoint Boulevard
New Castle, DE 19720
302-326-4802

Donvier nonelectric ice-cream makers, ice-cream and ice-pop molds, scoops, and cooking and baking tools and utensils.

Edward & Sons Trading Company, Inc.

www.edwardandsons.com
P.O. Box 1326
Carpinteria, CA 93014
805-684-8500

Organic coconut milk, organic shredded dried coconut, organic ice cream cones, gluten-free ice cream cones, organic chocolate sprinkles, and naturally colored sprinkles.

Frontier Natural Products Co-op

www.frontiercoop.com
3021 78th Street
Norway, IA 52318
800-669-3275

Organic, non-irradiated herbs, spices, vanilla and other extracts, and fair-trade cocoa powder and sugar.

Gold Mine Natural Foods

www.goldminenaturalfood.com
7805 Arjons Drive
San Diego, CA 92126
800-475-3663

Matcha green tea powder and maple syrup.

Ice Cream Professionals

www.icecreamprofessional.com
c/o Kitchen Professionals, LLC
Hewitt, NJ 07421
888-233-2722

Many different ice-cream makers for home and professional use.

InterNatural Foods, LLC

www.internaturalfoods.com
300 Broadacres Drive
Bloomfield, NJ 07003
973-338-1499

Organic instant coffee, powdered coffee substitutes, and chocolate.

KitchenAid

www.kitchenaid.com
P.O. Box 218
St. Joseph, MI 49085
800-334-6889

Ice-cream makers (including ice-cream-making attachments for mixers), food processors, and blenders.

Mail Order Catalog for Healthy Eating

www.healthy-eating.com
P.O. Box 180
Summertown, TN 92126
800-695-2241

A wide range of natural and vegan food products, including dairy alternatives like soy whipped cream, Ener-G Egg Replacer, and milk substitutes. Also organic coconut milk, dairy-free chocolate chips, coffee substitutes, flours, grains, sweeteners, and much more.

NaturalCandyStore.com

www.naturalcandystore.com
1717 Solano Way Suite 26
Concord, CA 94520
800-875-2409

Vegan ice-cream cones, candy canes, cake decorations, and dessert toppings.

Pangea Vegan Products

www.veganstore.com
2381 Lewis Avenue
Rockville, MD 20851
800-340-1200

Vegan chocolate, chocolate sauce, white chocolate, marshmallows, and candies.

Rival

www.rivalproducts.com
c/o JCS/THG, LLC
13120 Jurupa Avenue
Fontana, CA 92337
800-323-9519

Ice-cream makers and milk-shake makers.

Tea Zone

www.teazonline.com
15A Elm Street
Somerville, MA 02143
617-628-3238

Matcha green tea powder, common and exotic teas, and tea-making supplies.

Williams-Sonoma

www.williams-sonoma.com
P.O. Box 379900
Las Vegas, NV 89137
877-812-6235

Ice-cream makers and other kitchen appliances, cookware, bakeware, glassware, and ice-cream-sandwich molds.

Vegan Essentials

www.veganessentials.com
1701 Pearl Street, Unit B
Waukesha, WI 53186

Vegan chocolate, brownies, truffles, marshmallows, and more.

index

Recipe titles appear in *italic* typeface.

raspberry(ies)
   Cake, Chocolate-, 74
   -Chocolate Mousse Bombe, 82
   Ice Cream, Chocolate-, 19
   Ice Cream, Low-Fat, 54
   -Rhubarb Crisp Sundae, 91
   -Rhubarb Sauce, 122
   Sauce, Fresh, 121
   Sherbet, Red, 48
   Sorbet, 68
   in terrine recipe, 88
   in *Triple Berry Ice Cream*, 41
   Yogurt Pops, Watermelon-, 95
Red, White, and Blue Granola Bombe,
   85
Red, White, and Blue Parfait Sundae,
   90
Red Raspberry Sherbet, 48
red wine, in sorbet recipe, 68
rhubarb
   Crisp Sundae, Raspberry-, 91
   Sauce, Raspberry-, 122
   Sorbet, Strawberry-, 64
rice milk, 6
Ripple Ice Cream, Butterscotch, 11
Rocky Road Ice Cream, 17
Rosemary Ice Cream, 31
rum
   in ice cream recipe, 53
   Raisin Ice Cream, 24
   in sorbet recipe, 70

s

Sandwich Cookie Crust, 80
Sandwiches, Chocolate-Dipped Ice
   Cream, 104
sauce(s)
   Almond Hot Fudge, 116
   Butterscotch, 118
   Cherry-Ginger Terrine with Lemon,
   88
   Chocolate, 117
   Chunky Apple, 119
   Chunky Peach, 120
   Coconut Cream, 123

fresh
   Mango, 122
   Raspberry, 121
   Strawberry, 119
   Hardening Chocolate, 118
   Hot Fudge, 116
   Mint Hot Fudge, 116
   Orange Hot Fudge, 116
   for sundaes, 91
   White Chocolate, 117
   White Chocolate-Orange, 117
shakes
   Almond Dream, 109
   Blueberry, 109
   Chocolate, 108
    -Almond, 108
    -Hazelnut, 108
    -Mint, 108
    Peanut-Butter, 108
   Coffee, 110
   Kahlúa Coffee, 110
   Mocha, 110
   Peach, 109
   Ultimate Strawberry, 109
   Very Vanilla, 107
sherbets
   Lemon-Lime, 48
   Orange, 49
   Piña Colada, 50
   Pineapple, 50
   Red Raspberry, 48
   Tangerine, 49
   Terrine, Rainbow, 88
slicing ice cream desserts, 71
slushy(ies)
   alcohol in, 106
   Margarita, 106
   Watermelon, 106
Snowballs, 102
sodas
   Chocolate Ice Cream, 111
   Coffee Ice Cream, 112
   Mocha Ice Cream, 112
   Strawberry Ice Cream, 112
   Vanilla Ice Cream, 111
sorbets

Apricot, 65
Blueberry, 67
Blueberry-Banana, 67
Cantaloupe, 66
Cherry, 65
Cranberry-Orange, 69
Honeydew, 66
Kiwi, 60
Lemon, 62
   Daiquiri, 62
   Thyme, 63
Lime, 63
Mango, 68
Orange, 61
Pomegranate-Strawberry, 64
Raspberry, 68
Spiced Apple, 70
Strawberry, 61
   Daiquiri, 61
   Lemonade, 62
   -Rhubarb, 64
Tango-Mango, 69
soymilk, 7
Spiced Apple Sorbet, 70
Spice Ice Cream, Pumpkin, 32
Spicy Pecans, 125
spirits (alcohol), 8. *See also* specific
   types of
storing ice creams, 1–2
strawberry(ies)
   -Banana Ice Cream, 38
   -Banana Ice Cream, Low-Fat, 53
   in bombe recipe, 85
   Chiffon Pie, 73
   Cream Pops, 98
   Daiquiri Sorbet, 61
   Frozen Yogurt, 56
   Ice Cream, 38
    Low-Fat, 52
    Soda, 112
   Lemonade Pie, 73
   Lemonade Sorbet, 62
   Pops, Pomegranate-, 95
   -Rhubarb Sorbet, 64
   Sauce, Fresh, 119
   Shake, Ultimate, 109

ICE CREAM RULES!

Cathe Olson is a wife and mother, as well as a writer and natural foods cook. She has studied nutrition and cookery, both formally and informally, for over fifteen years, specializing in vegetarian, macrobiotic, and whole food diets. Cathe has cooked at natural food restaurants and delis in both the San Francisco Bay and Central Coast areas of California. She is the author of *The Vegetarian Mother's Cookbook* and *Simply Natural Baby Food* and has had articles published in national magazines such as *Mothering*, *Natural Family Online*, and *Natural Awakenings*. She writes the "Whole Family" column for *VegFamily Magazine* and reviews books for the *Journal of Agriculture & Food Information*.

Cathe is passionate about helping parents make nutritious food choices for themselves and their families. She is a frequent speaker at parenting classes, schools, natural food stores, libraries, and wellness centers. Her blog (http://catheolson.blogspot.com) offers information on healthful eating, organic food, genetic engineering, treatment of farm animals, book reviews, and more.

You can contact Cathe through her website at:
www.simplynaturalbooks.com.

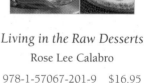